SCI

JAN 0 7 2010

D0438299

2010
2×2/11 8/11

Other books by Gostick and Elton

The Carrot Principle
The Daily Carrot Principle
The Invisible Employee
A Carrot a Day
The 24 Carrot Manager

Books by Gostick and Dana Telford

The Integrity Advantage

Book by Gostick and Scott Christopher

The Levity Effect

THE
ORANGE
REVOLUTION

How One Great Team
Can Transform an Entire Organization

Adrian Gostick
and Chester Elton

3 1336 08529 5732

FREE PRESS

New York   London   Toronto   Sydney

FREE PRESS
A Division of Simon & Schuster, Inc.
1230 Avenue of the Americas
New York, NY 10020

Copyright © 2010 by O.C. Tanner Company

All rights reserved, including the right to reproduce this book
or portions thereof in any form whatsoever. For information address
Free Press Subsidiary Rights Department, 1230 Avenue of the Americas,
New York, NY 10020

First Free Press hardcover edition September 2010.

FREE PRESS and colophon are trademarks of Simon & Schuster, Inc.

For information about special discounts for bulk purchases,
please contact Simon & Schuster Special Sales at 1-866-506-1949
or business@simonandschuster.com.

The Simon & Schuster Speakers Bureau can bring authors
to your live event. For more information or to book an event contact
the Simon & Schuster Speakers Bureau at 1-866-248-3049 or visit
our website at www.simonspeakers.com.

Manufactured in the United States of America

1 3 5 7 9 10 8 6 4 2

Library of Congress Cataloging-in-Publication Data
Gostick, Adrian Robert.
The orange revolution : how one great team can transform
an entire organization / Adrian Gostick and Chester Elton.—
1st free press hardcover ed.
p. cm.
1. Teams in the workplace. 2. Incentive awards—United States.
3. Employee motivation—United States. I. Elton, Chester. II. Title.
HD66.G674 2010
658.4'022—dc22
2010006091

ISBN 978-1-4391-8245-1
ISBN 978-1-4391-9666-3 (ebook)

Every great team has a great leader.
To one of the best we've ever known:
Dave Petersen.

CONTENTS

*"A small group of thoughtful people
could change the world.
Indeed, it's the only thing that ever has."*

—Margaret Mead

THE
ORANGE
REVOLUTION

1

Breakthrough Teams

It was 1:30 a.m. on Sunday, October 22, 1879, and experimenter Francis Jehl was still at work. He had been at his desk for ten hours, hunched over, carefully evacuating the air from a pear-shaped lightbulb. It wasn't an unusual workday for him. His boss's log routinely noted curious work habits: "we worked all night" or "32 continuous hrs." or "60 hrs." or "six days this week."

In fact "the Old Man," as "the boys" affectionately called their boss even before his hair turned gray, preferred to work at night when the team would not be interrupted by distracting visitors. As a result, Jehl often began work at 7:00 p.m. and continued until 7:00 the next morning.

"We work all night experimenting," lead experimenter Charles Batchelor wrote to his brother, Tom, "and sleep 'til noon in the day. We have got 54 different things on the carpet and some we have been on for four or five years. [My boss] is an indefatigable worker and there is no kind of failure, however disastrous, that affects him."

As Jehl finished removing the air from the bulb, the Old Man called his glassblower, Ludwig Boehm, to fully seal off its base. Over his head, twelve telegraph wires formed an intricate spider's web, all ending at a large battery at the center of the room.

Placing the bulb on a test stand, the Old Man connected

it to the nearby battery. Suddenly, the room was awash with light that illuminated work tables, machinery, and jars of chemicals on glass shelves lining the walls. The men quickly fell into the usual laboratory routine to observe the light's brightness and steadiness. They waited to record the moment when it finally burned out. But this experiment played out differently than ever before. While earlier filaments had burned out within several hours, the carbonized sewing thread that Batchelor had carefully threaded into the bulb stayed lit. As the hours passed, team members came and went: head machinist John Kruesi, who translated sketches into working devices; Francis Upton, the American scientific researcher who proved the concept mathematically; and John Lawson and Martin Force, laboratory assistants. Each of them felt a growing excitement at having earned a front-row seat to the historic event. They understood better than anyone else the difficulty—and benefits—of earning a place on the Old Man's team. The Old Man's name? Thomas Alva Edison.

On October 22, the remarkable bulb dreamed up by Edison, drawn by Batchelor, mathematically proved by Upton, built by Kruesi and Boehm, and tested by Lawson, Force, and Jehl, burned for thirteen and a half hours, with a light described by the New York *Herald*'s Marshal Fox as, "the mellow sunset of an Italian autumn . . . a little globe of sunshine, a veritable Aladdin's lamp," before Edison determined he had seen enough. "If it will burn that number of hours now, I know I can make it burn a hundred!" he cried exultantly.

If you were asked who invented incandescent electric light, and you answered Edison, you'd be right and you'd be wrong. The revolution that Edison wrought was the product of a team. That's how he thought of it, and that's how the team thought of it. For some reason, it's easier for us to assign credit to a single person than to a team. We love the idea of a lone genius, the mastermind, the hero. From an early age, we're indoctrinated with the single-achiever ideal in school. Our textbooks boil things down to their simplest form, and for a fifth-grader, it's easy to say that Edison = lightbulbs.

The reality is very different. Here's what geniuses do: they build great teams.

Never intimidated by other great minds, Edison actively sought out men with a broad base of knowledge, a passion for learning, impeccable character, and a commitment to excellence. He then organized them into small teams comprised of an experimenter and two or three assistants. They were given a goal and allowed to pursue it independently. The story is told that once, when an experimenter asked Edison what he would do with a particularly difficult problem, Edison replied, "Don't ask me. If I knew, I would try it myself!"

That's not to say Edison didn't care about the process: quite the opposite. He was intensely interested, neglecting sleep and personal hygiene to pursue his inventions. Edison was known to "flit" around the factory in a black floppy-rimmed sombrero and dirty suit with his hair uncombed, checking in on his teams of experimenters—examining and instructing, but rarely interfering. He recognized that by allowing each of the talented people he'd assembled to stretch and succeed independently of him, he got the best results.

As Edison explained: "I generally instructed them on the general idea of what I wanted carried out, and when I came across an assistant who was in any way ingenious, I sometimes refused to help him out in his experiments, telling him to see if he could not work it out himself, so as to encourage him."

Unbelievably, Edison—one of the most brilliant minds in the world—had accepted that he alone did not possess all the answers; but together, his team usually did.

Edison shared the vision, the work, the fun—and the rewards—with his team. One lab assistant described his work as "strenuous but joyous." In a letter to his father, Upton wrote, "The strangest thing to me is the $12 that I get each Saturday, for my labor does not seem like work, but like study." Key team members received shares in Edison's companies and he let them invest in the projects to which they contributed. Perhaps most significant, when the time came to expand operations, Edison rewarded members of his team with leadership positions at the new companies, enabling many of them to retire wealthy men.

Recent research confirms the wisdom of Edison's approach to collaboration. University of New Mexico professor Vera John-Steiner explains that collaboration enables people to compensate "for each other's blind spots. . . . Collaboration operates through a process in which the successful intellectual achievements of one person arouse the intellectual passions and enthusiasms of others."

In the early 1970s Kenneth Bruffee, an English and composition professor, introduced the then-radical argument that students learned more through group work than when listening only to their teacher. And collaboration has also been shown to benefit the almighty buck. Mark Potter, along with his colleagues Richard T. Bliss at Babson College, and Christopher Schwarz at University of California at Irvine, set out to discover the best management approach when it came to mutual funds success.

"It's fascinating," Potter told us. "If you're wondering where the safest place is for your money—a team-managed approach is much less risky." In their research, Potter and his colleagues measured three thousand equity mutual funds over a twelve-year period. They not only found less risk with the team approach, but as counterintuitive as it sounds, the total cost of owning a team-managed mutual fund is nearly fifty basis points lower annually than a mutual fund managed by an individual.

This is just a sampling of the research that has come out in recent years regarding the power of collaboration. It coincided with technological advances that created the emergence of linked teams that could communicate faster and cheaper than could previously be imagined. Motivated by the data and the possibility of virtual, global teams, leaders have increasingly turned to teamwork to save their floundering organizations, but only in the most superficial way; and that's the rub.

Rather than fundamentally change how we work and interact, we've merely changed our vocabulary. It's hard not to notice how the use of "team" in corporate-speak has exploded over the past ten years; and along the way, its true meaning and power has been hijacked, as in, "Attention team members: cleanup on aisle four."

Instead of referencing power and transformation, "team" has become the default word for "employee." It is the propagandist's cynical coercion: "Let's call them teams; then they'll get along better." There is nothing about the true meaning of teamwork in its casual usage. There's a missing link. Something's not working.

When "team" is used as simply another business buzzword—"let's drill down and grab a take-away in this space and take it back to the team"—it diminishes what the powerful word (and concept) can really achieve.

It's gone so far that many teams in today's companies are not true teams at all; they're faux. Organizationally, structurally, motivationally, they are not set up to work together effectively. They're simply vague labels placed on random groupings, or even the entire organization as a whole. And those labels accomplish nothing. Someone has told leadership that they should have teams, and so they have them. But employees are not fooled. They continue to be groups or departments of people that simply have the blanket of "team" thrown upon them. Take a peek underneath and you'll find a group of individuals largely fending for themselves.

The sad truth for leadership is that they are adrift at sea. They're expected to motivate people to work like high-performance teams, often without having experienced teamwork themselves. So they fake it. They use the training and vocabulary of teams and hope for the best. Then, when their people fail to bring down big game, managers throw up their hands in frustration: "What's wrong with these people?"

The problem isn't necessarily with the people, but with what they're being asked to do: work together without the necessary relationship tools or the guidelines that provide focus. Addressing this gap of understanding and application is our purpose. Over the past two decades we've traveled the world, seeking out exceptional teams that are transforming their entire organizations in all types of businesses. We watched how these teams functioned, how they interacted on the job and off, how they were managed, and how they were motivated. Along the way, we collected their stories. And then we noticed how often we were repeating these stories to companies, managers, and employees who were struggling to align their teams with the right outcomes. These teams knew the treasure existed—they just didn't have a legible map. That's when we realized these stories were too good not to share.

You'll meet many of them in the coming pages, including Rajendra "Guru" Gursahaney and his remarkable team at Pepsi Beverages Company who developed a process that will transform the way the world drinks bottled beverages, all while saving his company more than $7 million a year in plastics costs. You'll learn of Scott O'Neil's creative marketing team that redefined the National Basketball Association after the retirement of superstar Michael Jordan and set four years of league attendance records. We'll tell you the story of the U.S. Foodservice team that created a measured approach to grow market share and brought millions and millions in new revenue into the company . . . during a recession.

We're convinced these stories will inspire you; and we'll

back them up with empirical research from the Best Companies Group, which creates the "Best Places to Work" lists for newspapers, magazines, and television. The Best Companies Group's database features more than 350,000 participants from twenty-eight industries. The most exciting part about this data is that it was collected during the worst recession in our working lives, allowing us to get a glimpse of teams functioning (and producing results) under the most challenging circumstances.

What we found was unexpected—and eye-opening. We were able to statistically establish a pattern of characteristics displayed by members of the best teams, as well as a set of rules that great teams live by. Even more rewarding was the realization that these qualities could be shared with other teams, like yours.

So, what sparks the first moments of a revolutionary team? What directs their journey down the road least traveled? And what awaits when you unlock the potential of true teamwork? All these questions have clear-cut answers and follow a surprisingly regimented process. First, these teams share a belief in their own ability to write the future. After all, it is people in the trenches, not senior leaders, who are the true force behind any sustained change in a company. Great teams universally reject the long-held view of the individual genius or charismatic CEO changing an organization, and instead place their faith fully in themselves and their ability to achieve.

It's a big leap of faith for a group of regular people to make, even on a good day; but it was this very type of belief in themselves, rather than their leaders, that saved the lives of one breakthrough team in the middle of the Indian Ocean seven years ago.

Like most crises, no one saw it coming. And yet when water started rushing through the submarine's hull, Able Seaman Geordie Bunting of the Royal Australian Navy

(RAN) knew enough to realize that he was probably going to die.

Bunting had spent his shift working in the small, lower motor room of the Collins-class submarine HMAS *Dechaineux*. As he worked over heavy machinery, he was constantly aware of his fifty-four crewmates above him, going about the continuous six-hour-on six-hour-off routine of the submarine crew: the off-crew either asleep in their racks, watching movies, or playing Monopoly; the on-crew monitoring the ocean around them via headsets and screens—everyone within a few feet of each other at all times.

Bunting knew these people like his own family. He knew their birthdays, their middle names, their kids' names, their habits and histories. And when he heard the ear-deafening bang and saw the water pour into the motor room, he immediately knew they were in serious trouble.

Like all submariners, Bunting understood that if the *Dechaineux* was at a shallow depth and became damaged, he and his crewmates had a chance to escape using free ascent from an airlock. But in deeper waters the hope of rescue was almost nonexistent. Even if a diving bell could be brought in, it could take weeks to rescue the crew, and by then, the air supply would be long gone.

As fate would have it, on February 12, 2003, the *Dechaineux* had dived to its maximum depth, well below six hundred feet, in an attempt to test its systems under full pressure. And that pressure had proved to be too much. A flexible sea hose burst. Within ten seconds, enough seawater had poured into the motor room to toss Bunting around like he was in a washing machine.

Ironically, while most Royal Australian Navy recruits go through Hull Training, which simulates conditions exactly like this, submariners are exempt from the exercise. The reasoning is that if a submarine takes on water, the craft is not salvageable. Bunting, suddenly caught in that very situation, had a hard time disagreeing.

"It was coming in so fast, I thought it was all over," he said. With water up to his neck, and nearly unconscious, Bunting immediately understood that so far under the ocean surface, there was no one to save him and the rest of the crew but *themselves*.

Meanwhile, outside the motor room, the crew instantly sprang into action, triggering an emergency override, which shut down all the external valves and stopped the water intake. Other crew members rushed to the flooded motor room, fished Seaman Bunting out by his lapel, and slammed the door shut. The water level wasn't rising, but they all knew that at this depth, the amount of water they had taken on could very well send them to the bottom.

This far under the surface, dropping just a little lower, "would have been like crushing an empty Coke can in your hand," said Bunting of the water pressure that would have collapsed the vessel. "We were too deep to hit the bottom alive."

Working quickly and with precision, the crew adjusted the controls to increase speed and the rate of ascent. At the same time, they blew out the ballast and lightened the load. Then they held their breath and waited; but the submarine did not respond.

In that dreadful moment, most crew members said they thought of the 118 Russian submariners who had died just three years earlier in the Barents Sea. On that fateful day, an onboard torpedo exploded during maneuvers. Russian Navy Lieutenant-Captain Dmitry Kolesnikov was one of just twenty-three of the 118 crewmen to survive the initial explosion, only to later succumb to cold and carbon dioxide poisoning, trapped inside the hull of the crippled nuclear submarine on the ocean's floor.

While waiting for a rescue that never came, twenty-seven-year-old Kolesnikov scrawled an almost illegible final message to his wife: "It's too dark to write here, but I will try to do it blindly. It looks like there is no chance—ten to twenty percent. Here is a list of personnel who are in the ninth section and trying to get out. Hello to everyone, do not despair."

Known as the "the note," Kolesnikov's last words are infamous among submariners around the world. Many have the words memorized. Some have nightmares about them.

Fortunately for Bunting and crew, after a short hesitation the *Dechaineux* began slowly to respond to the crew's frantic efforts. Working every tactic, the crew began to inch the craft upward. Soon, the submarine was rising at twice its normal rate of ascent. A few men laughed nervously as they heard cups sliding off tables in the mess hall and clattering to the floor.

Still, it took three long minutes for the submarine to surface—an eternity to the desperate crew members. After reaching daylight, their ordeal wasn't over; they faced the very real possibility that the submarine would sink before they could reach Perth, a full eight hours away. There was little they could do but pray that the hull would hold.

"It was pretty bloody close, mate," said Bunting. And he wasn't exaggerating. Investigators later determined that had the *Dechaineux* continued to flood for just a further twenty seconds, the sub and its crew would have sunk to the bottom of the Indian Ocean.

"It changed my life," said Bunting. "Another five seconds and we would have been in big trouble . . . another ten and you have got to question whether we could have surfaced."

Twenty seconds. That was the difference between life and death.

In the midst of the crisis that threatened their lives, the Aussie crew acted like a real team, the kind that makes us tear up in movies and throw our popcorn into the air at football games. No one argues with that. But let's examine that statement more closely. What did they do, exactly, that proved their teamwork? In the face of disaster, the submariners responded quickly and protected each other. They rescued those in immediate danger. They thought creatively to solve a problem. They functioned as a support for each other, keeping cool when things looked bad.

On the technical side, they adjusted controls to right the situation. They jettisoned the ballast and lightened the load with the hopes that the sub would respond. Certainly they were following their training. There was no time to consult the sub's owner's manual. Twenty seconds were all they had. They acted and then crossed their fingers.

Here's something they didn't do: call the commander and ask what he thought. That's something worth mentioning. It's what makes this story revolutionary as an example of teamwork. In the wake of the disaster, the sailors of *Dechaineux* did not resort to a hierarchy of leadership, no coach on the sideline calling the final play of the game.

"I was proud of them the day before, and I was proud of them the day after," said Commander Pete Scott. "On the day itself, I did nothing, the ship's company did everything. They identified the problem, they reacted to the problem, they did everything they needed to and we got to the surface."

According to the commander, the men didn't wait for him to give orders or save them; *they* saved the ship. And they were ready to do it. Each member of the crew was extremely proficient at his job, and each trusted the others implicitly, and each was ready to sacrifice for the whole.

Now, we're not saying that the managers of teams don't make a difference—or even that top management doesn't play a vital role. In fact, we will show later how leaders can do a great deal to build such highly functioning teams. But the fact is that people in breakthrough teams report their highest loyalty is their relationship with one another—the other team members.

Vince Lombardi explained it like this when asked why sports teams win. "[It's] because the players love one another." Love's a loaded word. We'll stop short of advocating love in business.

What our research clearly reveals is that within the most productive teams, employees feel a heightened sense of camaraderie, considering at least one of their co-workers a close friend. They also feel their manager cares about their well-being, a dramatically human emotion. For those who prefer numbers, 63 percent of workers found office productivity to be positively affected when co-workers are friends outside of work. All these indicators clearly point to camaraderie, or even love if you choose to call it that, as a major driver of esprit de corps, which in turn drives productivity and achievement.

Max Messmer, chairman of Accountemps, says, "Colleagues who are friends are more likely to support one another when presented with challenges or new responsibilities, enhancing workflow and team spirit. Those who are able to form friendships early on the job are likely to acclimatize quickly and stay on board for the long term."

Edison's Menlo Park team was a model of such esprit de corps. Some of it was pure silliness. The factory on the hill where the lightbulb was created housed a small organ where the men would sit together during midnight breaks and make up little ditties about their boss and their job while sharing smoked herring and hard crackers:

> *"I am the Wizard of the electric light*
> *And a wide-awake Wizard, too.*
> *I see you're rather bright and appreciate the might*
> *Of what I daily do."*

The men worked together and played together and shared the same goals—establishing an immense esprit de corps that carried them through the discouraging times and toward eventual success.

And yet as close as Edison was to his teammates, he did

not enjoy visits from outsiders, even those who might invest in his work. He complained that each morning, the appearance of visitors would bring a night of productive work to an abrupt end. He described dreading the appearance of the "line of heads" climbing up the hill every morning to "devour" his time, so much dreading the intrusion that he expressed relief when a tornado and dramatic rain storm once arrived, because it spared him from visitors.

His attitude might have been a little extreme, but not unique. Breakthrough teams regularly report feeling conflicted about the demands of senior leadership, shareholders, or other outside forces. They don't set out to to rock the boat, but at times they realize the boat is going in the wrong direction. Because of this, many of the teams we met were at one point or another at odds with their bosses. Some had even ignored customer research or short-term shareholder gain in their drive to do what they thought was right for the organization long-term. They are not determined to be difficult, just to be the best, and that requires what we define as an Orange mind-set.

Let us explain this term.

Over the last few years, our series of business books has focused on "carrots," our catchphrase for employee recognition. We even created a system to help managers understand and implement the powerful tools of motivation, engagement, recognition, and appreciation.

Since then, our research has come to show us that the same practices of appreciation and recognition that create revolutionary leaders also contribute to the success of breakthrough teams. Since carrots are a foundational part of the formula for team growth and achievement, we use the term "Orange" to describe the overall characteristics, rules, and behaviors of great teams.

The word "Orange" has been connected with more than a few revolutionary events in history. While most recently linked to election protests in the Ukraine, there have also been Orange uprisings in Ireland, China, England, and the Netherlands.

These revolutions signal a transition—a spirited quest driven by people to improve the world around them. And whether a transformation actually occurred or not, one aspect of these historical events deserves acknowledgment—each revolution, right or wrong, was inspired by the passion of individuals: people who raised a rallying flag of Orange, believing it was the color of change.

In business, an Orange Revolution possesses that same depth of passion. However, the intent is not to topple a regime. Instead, this Orange Revolution begins in the hearts of team members—focused on conquering barriers, expectations, and stagnancy.

Breakthrough teams understand that important work relationships require effort. In the interest of the greater good, team members agree to set standards for their interactions. Rather than feel restrictive, team members report that a code of personal and team conduct kicks the door wide open to possibilities, where success and rewards inevitably follow, unfettered by petty interpersonal problems. In a breakthrough team, each member agrees to:

- **Demonstrate personal competency.** Edison made determining such competency the first order of business upon meeting a potential new employee. Of course, you could make a good case that personal competence alone does not create an automatic winner. Think of athletic Dream Teams that are not the sum of their individual parts. Talent alone does not propel a team to greatness.

    Think of teams where some members withhold their full ability. An implied contract is broken, conflict typically ensues, and sometimes it's quite dramatic. Take, for example, a highly profitable steel mill in the United States, where a fed-up team of steel line workers drove an underperforming teammate off the line with red-hot rods. Certainly extreme, but in Nucor's performance culture, personal competence is required. Not by management, but by peers. It's hot, dirty work and it takes a team to do it right. And those who don't measure up may, quite literally, find themselves on the wrong end of the stick.

- **Expand their competency with leadership traits of goal setting, communication, trust, accountability (what we call the Basic 4), and recognition.** The Wharton School of Business and Gartner research firm once polled a group of senior leaders on why they thought their big ideas didn't get implemented. Interestingly, many of the top obstacles related to neglect of leadership basics by managers and their employees: (1) poor or inadequate information sharing between people and business units responsible for execution (communication); (2) unclear communication of responsibility and/or accountability for execution decisions or actions (communication, accountability); (3) lack of feeling of "ownership" of a strategy or execution plans among employees (goal setting, accountability); and (4) an inability to generate "buy in" agreement on critical execution steps or actions (communication, trust). The research demonstrates the critical nature of a few foundational rules of leadership, as does pure common sense. If as an individual, I set clear goals with my manager and teammates, if I communicate openly and honestly, if I do what I say I will do and build trust, and if I hold myself accountable for hitting my goals, logic says I will be valued and appreciated. However, a lack in any of these areas will derail a team member, and can ultimately derail an entire team.

  As for the role of recognition, a ten-year study conducted for us by HealthStream Research shows that strong teams report receiving high levels of recognition not only from their managers but also from their fellow team members, which is unheard of within lower-performing teams. Because everyone is cheering for each other, they also report recognition happening more frequently, with more celebrations at not only the end of projects or when goals are reached, but also at smaller milestones along the way. And best of all, we were able to correlate this type of appreciation to much stronger business results, including financial performance more than three times higher than in organizations without a culture of recognizing excellence.

- **Clearly visualize the cause.** While every member of a high-performing team serves a unique role, members never lose sight of the big picture. This creates a focus that guides their cumulative effort to shared achievement. We often think of creative, world-changing teams as functioning biologically, like living cells. Cells create organs. Organs produce organisms. Organisms combine to form organizations. And if the cells in the heart don't understand where they fit into the common cause, their function—at all levels—will be impaired.

- Follow *The Rule of 3.*
  - **Wow**—Breakthrough Teams commit to a standard of world-class performance.
  - **No Surprises**—All team members are accountable for openness and honest debate, and each knows what to expect from the others.
  - **Cheer**—Team members support, recognize, appreciate, and cheer others and the group on to victory.

We capture the ideas in what we call the Orange Revolution Model:

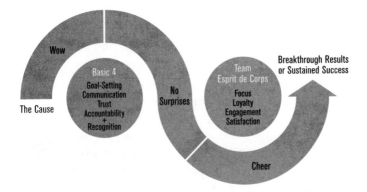

The most important thing about the model is that it takes only the lightest touch by a leader to maintain success. To facilitate this type of team, motivated and skilled leaders:

Ensure the right people join. Great managers insist on finding the necessary personnel and help the team consider candidates for their technical skills, integrity, empathy, personality, and, of course, for their ability to work well with the rest of the team.

Translate corporate goals. By helping employees understand the big picture and their collective role in furthering the cause, managers help lead the team toward goals with the most impact.

Facilitate rule setting. Effective managers help pave the revolutionary road by gathering their teams to establish a collective code of conduct that will become the blueprint for all decisions and interactions.

Promote a culture of appreciation. Not only do great leaders recognize above-and-beyond achievements, they also facilitate peer-to-peer recognition and make their teams visible to those around the organization.

This is a far cry from the list most leaders draw up when asked about their duties. We find that the majority of managers' attention is spent focused on completing their own work or addressing the needs of clients and senior management. The majority of managers still view themselves as either the senior "doer" on a team, or as the task master who gives daily assignments. On the other hand, within an Orange Revolution model their primary role is as facilitators who smooth the pathway forward.

Marilynn Brewer first described the type of give-and-take relationship that is evolving between breakthrough teams and their leaders a decade ago in the *Journal of Social Issues*. She called it obligatory interdependence. It's a fancy name for a simple concept: to survive as a species, human beings must learn to depend on each other. Translated to business, the rule of the jungle is: A leader can't go it alone.

Bruce Coslett was on the same track when he described the future of American football: "The era of the rugged individual is giving way to the era of the team player." He didn't know he might well have been describing the trajectory of the manager's gatekeeper role in business, but it's true. Leaders of revolutionary teams must begin to see themselves as playing a role on the team rather than as someone outside and above their colleagues.

Not surprisingly, when many managers first see this role change it can spark worries about the diminishment of the contribution of the leader. Won't they suffer a loss of status and ownership?

Here's the twist: **The more power managers give to their employees, the more those employees esteem their leaders.** In our 200,000-person research study published in *The Carrot Principle*, we found that when managers built strong team cultures focused on recognition and member engagement, employee ratings of their managers' skills at goal setting, communication, trust, and accountability soared. In modern revolutionary teams, the interdependent relationship of leaders and employees means everyone wins.

Rudyard Kipling spelled it out succinctly and poetically in his classic *The Jungle Book*:

The strength of the pack is the wolf,
And the strength of the wolf is the pack.

This begs the question of why leaders would ever work against the success of their teams, since it undermines their own personal success. Sadly, most leaders undermine their teams unwittingly, simply by conforming to in-vogue management practices.

Unbelievably, in the corporate world, it has become common practice to share skill sets between areas by reassigning employees every two years. The result is total disruption of any camaraderie that might be developing within a group. Overly optimistic leaders believe that employees should feel esprit de corps for the organization as a whole, not a certain department. Unfortunately, that's typically not realistic. Few people bond with a soulless organization or senior leaders they see only a few times a year, and few employees feel even a Herculean effort on their part would have an impact on the organization as a whole. Since the earliest human history, we have bonded first with those immediately around us, those we work and play with every day.

So when we clear-cut a department, and break up a highly functioning team, we also sever the esprit de corps that has been developing over years between the people in that group. That kind of trust and chemistry doesn't spring back up overnight. It takes time to grow.

Knowing this, it's no wonder as many as 40 percent of senior people fail in new roles; their support network has been pulled out from under them. In contrast, however, the vast majority succeed when they are transferred as part of a team.

Fortunately, some companies are beginning to recognize the role of team dynamics in achievement. Nokia, for example, moves entire teams when it needs to share skill sets, thereby maintaining relationships and the revolutionary spirit that powers innovation and benefits everyone, including leadership. Online retailer Zappos encourages teams to laugh and bond together—while they're still on the clock. Around the world, we've been privileged to document the successes of companies, like these, that are waking up to the value of camaraderie in achieving business results.

Still, skeptics remain; and, really, who can blame them? The hype about teamwork through the years turned out to be much ado about nothing. If you harbor some doubts yourself about the value of team-building efforts, let us introduce some eye-opening findings captured during our fall 2008 global study by Towers Perrin (now Towers Watson). Look what happens to employee engagement when teamwork is more than lip service, when we make commitments to interact and work differently, when we let go of the old way of seeing things and view our role at work in a new way.

Percent of Employees Who Are Engaged

Global Average	When motivated by working in teams	When I had a recent recognition in front of team/ department	When I understand how my team contributes to the success of the organization
64%	68%	70%	75%

At the left, the 64 percent engagement number shows us that today, some 36 percent of the global working population is not personally invested in their work. In short, they don't care. But see how the number of engaged workers increases when employees are organized into motivating teams, increases again when members of the team cheer and recognize each other, and increases to 75 percent when team members understand the big picture and how their work impacts it? Feeling part of an authentic team that cheers for each other and has clear goals leads to higher engagement wherever you are in the world, from Brazil to Germany, Singapore to Mexico.

We have been lucky enough to see, firsthand, the immense power of breakthrough teams illustrated during our travels. As you continue to read, you'll get to see that power as we did. One of our favorites was the maverick team that decided it could reduce manufacturing time from one week to one day. Instantly a new standard was set for all to follow. In another organization, a customer service team showed an entire organization the new mark of excellence in product knowledge. Overnight, R&D, marketing, and distribution were inspired by new perspectives on old products, methods, or policies. Within a large restaurant chain, one small group introduced new menu items and process improvements that the entire chain adopted, followed by every one of their competitors, changing an entire industry for the better.

In *The Orange Revolution*, we've laid out the revolutionary road to creating such breakthrough teams for you. We hope you'll use this book in a number of ways to create your own story:

- As a profit finder—engaging the people and teams that already exist to enhance the strength of a company.
- As an organizer—giving you the steps to structure teams that will realize their hidden potential and create extraordinary results.
- As a possibility guide—opening a collective thought process between team members, employees and managers, and executives and staff about the potential of synergistic teams and leveraged strengths.
- As a reference manual—spotlighting the successes of other teams and providing easy-to-follow "how-to" applications.

You say you want a revolution? We all want to change the world, right, even if it's just our part of it? And the amazing thing is that you absolutely can. You just can't do it alone.

2

The Common Cause

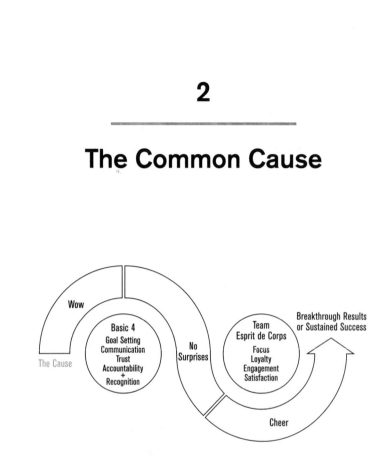

It was December 31, 1776, just five days after American General George Washington's military coup at Trenton, New Jersey. The British Redcoats were stunned. After a series of American losses, it seemed the tide of the war was about to turn. And yet the men of Washington's triumphant army were heading home.

It was ludicrous, really. Washington's success in leading 2,400 troops across the icy Delaware River in the middle of the night, amid pouring rain, to launch a surprise attack on the sleeping Hessians at Trenton, had provided a significant victory for the struggling revolutionary forces. The battle

22

was so important, in fact, that it would later be considered the turning point of the Revolutionary War.

But for Washington's men, hunkered down in freezing temperatures, none of that was very clear. Instead, they saw that already a full 90 percent of the original revolutionary troops were gone. Many had been killed in battle, but large numbers were deserting every day, feeling the cause for independence was lost.

The men who remained were not deserters. They had loyally followed their leader across the river. They had fought valiantly on Breed's Hill, at White Plains, Kip's Bay, and other sites. They had done everything they had been asked to do up until now. But due to an odd statute in the conscription laws, every man's enlistment was up the next day, on January 1, 1777—and none of them intended to stay a single minute past that deadline.

The way they all saw it, by the grace of God, they had been given an easy and honorable way to exit what many now believed was a losing cause, and they were taking it. This meant that for all intents and purposes, just when the tide was turning in the Americans' favor, the war was ending. The revolution had failed.

With this prospect looming before him, Washington gathered his men together on a ridge along the south side of the Assunpink Creek, with the Delaware River to the left and a brown wood to their right. Looking down from his high, white steed at the laborers, farmers, and tradesmen who made up his army, the general made them an offer he believed they could not resist: a $10 bonus to each man who would stay a few more months. Everyone on the hill that day understood this was a handsome sum; and Washington must have felt confident in his offer. He nodded to the drummer boys who began a rousing roll, then asked all who would take the bonus to step forward.

Not a single man moved. Time passed. The drum roll

faltered and stopped. Downcast, and perhaps a little angry, Washington wheeled his horse around and rode off. The wind howled over the frozen ground as the men remained in formation on the cold hill, and waited.

Among them was Nathanael Greene, who described what followed in a letter to Nicholas Cooke. According to Greene, in time General Washington returned to his men. This time, his overconfidence was gone and he spoke with great familiarity and affection, looking many of his men in the eye.

"My brave fellows, you have done all I asked you to do and more than could be reasonably expected, but your country is at stake, your wives, your houses, and all that you hold dear. You have worn yourselves out with fatigues and hardships, but we know not how to spare you. If you will consent to stay one month longer, you will render that service to the cause of liberty, and to your country, which you can probably never do under any other circumstance."

The general went on to say that he wished he could pass the burden of war to others, but there was no one to accept the charge. He urged the men to consider what they, and they only, could do. Asking them to think beyond themselves, to focus on the greater good, he promised that if they would stay and fight with him, their glorious cause would change the world.

Then he signaled for the drum roll to begin again. Seconds passed. Finally, one man stepped forward, then another, and another, until every single man on the field had committed. They were on their way to making their cause a reality.

Washington learned a valuable lesson that day, one that few in business ever really put into practice. Nothing else—not even bonuses or other perks—motivates like the opportunity to define and unite behind a common purpose.

You'd think this concept would come as a relief to all of

us with revolutionary tendencies, since it doesn't cost much of anything to define what we stand for; but the concept somehow scares us. We simply don't know how to go about implementing a common direction, and so we don't even try. The result is small-scale team anarchy, because in the absence of a defined overarching reason for being, members come up with their own agendas. The resulting mishmash of competing personal goals places teammates at cross purposes, triggers rivalries and turf wars, and can even prompt co-worker sabotage. In the most extreme cases, people desert their teams, either by leaving physically or by checking out mentally and emotionally. Either way, the cumulative costs for businesses are staggering.

The costs resulting from a lack of shared purpose are large enough to catch the attention of smart teams and the employees who depend on them for their livelihoods. Like the revolutionaries serving under Washington, breakthrough team members are coming to agreements on their cause and are uniting around their ability to make a difference. And they are doing it within a variety of larger corporate environments—structured and chaotic, supportive and obstructive.

In some teams the shared purpose arises from a conversation between a couple of members with a sincere need for clarity. The process they go through to hone their purpose is clear enough that it spreads to the rest of their group. In some cases it even spreads systemically. However, the cause for most teams is simply an adoption of the corporate reason for being. In these cases, the corporate mission is articulated by management and trickled down to workers.

Both approaches can work. But there is a preferred third method that generates the highest levels of employee engagement: Every person in the company has a small voice in deciding the overarching cause. And then every team defines what that cause means to their group, and then each person takes a turn envisioning how they can make a contribution to the team and company causes. Giving employees a voice in the cause gets everyone invested toward the same end—fueling pride and creating momentum that builds as team members reach milestones along the way.

Medical City Dallas Hospital is a marvelous illustration of the power of an entire organization working together to achieve such a common cause.

They say that everything's bigger in Texas, and this hospital is no exception. There's a reason, after all, that they call it a *city*. With 2,500 employees, 660 beds, 24,000 admissions a year, and 65,000 emergency room visits annually, it's a large place. So big, in fact, that a decade ago administration and staff alike say they lost their patient-focused direction.

"Ten years ago, we had the attitude, 'I replaced your knee, you should be happy,'" said Virginia Rose, vice president of strategic development. And that mind-set manifested itself in an often aloof demeanor. "Many staff members wouldn't even provide directions to our guests. In most cases all you would get was, 'go left, go right, go left again.' Employees certainly wouldn't take someone where they needed to go. They wouldn't talk to patients in elevators; it was silence as you went up or down. Staff answered the phones, 'Sixth South,' without any passion in their voice for providing service."

That lack of personal attention had taken its toll. By year 2000, Medical City was limping along with a 36 percent bed vacancy rate, a number matched by 36 percent annual employee turnover. Patient satisfaction on a national 4.0 scale was a very average 3.4. While their quality of medicine was undeniably cutting edge, their quality of compassion and respect was not. It began to look like the crack physicians and staff who could perform intricate heart, kidney, and stem-cell transplants, and even pull off some of the world's most complicated cranial-facial operations, might not be able to heal themselves.

But leadership had a vision: create a Medical City Experience that would make patients and their loved ones devotees of the hospital. Said Rose, "When you walk into a Starbucks you know what you are going to get. You align yourself with a certain experience. So for us, the question became: Why would people align themselves with Medical City?"

The answer wasn't that easy. "You've got to remember, it's health care. It's not real sexy," added Rose. "You come here because you have to come. But while you are here, how can we deliver such exquisite care and kindness that people would become raving fans? So if they or their families ever need health care, they come to Medical City."

Faced with this dilemma, CEO Britt Berrett understood the value of getting not only employees' buy-in but their input about how the hospital could go about executing on the promise. He tapped Rose to create a multidisciplined consortium of clinicians, administrators, and staff, later dubbed The Patient Promise Posse, who voluntarily worked together to come up with a plan to create a single-minded focus on patients and their families. But instead of barking out orders, the team decided their first order of business was to hold up a mirror, figuratively, to every employee and ask them to take a good, long look at themselves and how they served customers.

Remarking on where the hospital staff was versus where it had to go, Rose said, "Technically we were excellent, but warm and fuzzy we were not. That was when we said, 'It's okay to care. It's okay to cry. It's okay to say you are sorry. You don't have to be a robot.' Our promise would involve the family in decisions, show them that we cared. And that meant we had to change our attitude in how we were treating people."

Everyone on the Posse knew it would be a painful process, certainly not as easy as putting an article about the new focus in the newsletter, but they also understood that by doing this right they would be following a powerful method for engaging people and changing behavior. It was the only way to get the organization's buy-in to the process. So they bit the bullet and took on first the most intimidating group of all—upper management.

"We put our leadership through the admitting process. They had to wear gowns. They had to be wheeled around the hospital. We wanted them to see what it was like in a gown, with people staring down at you, to see what a patient sees. How do employees treat you? What does the signage say? It was eye-opening for them," said Rose.

The Posse didn't stop there. They went to the switchboard operators and asked if they could tape calls, and then played them back. "The operators laughed when they first heard themselves," she added. "But then they said, 'My gosh, I really am speaking fast.' We explained how you might think hurrying is making you more efficient, but it's actually making your customers ask more questions."

By far the most impactful thing they did was to create a series of videos featuring input from secret shoppers and patient comments. To put it mildly, the movies weren't pretty; but they kept the customer-care cause front and center.

"In one video, one of our physicians saw a confused gentleman in the hallway. Our secret shopper was nearby. The physician said, 'I hope you brought some bread crumbs,' and walked away. He didn't ask if he could help," said Rose.

Yet these criticisms were difficult for some to swallow at first. "We had some pushback at the start from some areas, especially among the doctors," Rose said. "But as the changes began around them, we were very honest with them. We said, 'We know you don't like seeing this about yourselves, but we need you to support the process. We need your input.'"

And Rose and her team weren't kidding about valuing everyone's input. After grabbing employee attention with the videos, the Posse communicated a challenge. "We asked each group in the hospital to develop three goals to get us to a higher level of patient satisfaction," she said.

The response was amazing; even the physicians came around quickly. Key physician leaders advocated to allow families into care areas like the emergency room, and presented their idea to other physicians, who despite some reservations, realized that this was a way of providing higher quality care that would lead to better outcomes and patient and family satisfaction. And it's worked. "We find that if family members are allowed into the emergency room while we are providing life-saving care, they are much more pleased than if we put them in the waiting room, no matter the outcome," said Rose.

In another instance, one of the doctors (a renowned pediatric cardiovascular surgeon who performs hundreds of intricate operations a year) assumed a tremendous personal responsibility to influence patient loyalty and helped design a process for better patient and family communication.

Hospital staff members also introduced out-of-the-box ideas such as auto detailing, banking, concierge services, and valet parking. Not to be outdone, the cafeteria reinvented itself as City Gourmet. No more reheating food in a microwave (as is typical in many hospitals). At Medical City, patients now order food as if they are staying in a hotel. As long as it's in their diet, patients can order anything from a gourmand steak to devilish chocolate thunder cake.

Interactions in the halls began to change. "We'll now take our patients where they need to go, even if it's walking them to another building," said Rose. "If an employee sees a visitor in the elevator, our people will talk about their care, the weather, or something to put them at ease. If someone looks lost, we'll ask if we can help."

Even the maintenance department got into the spirit,

down to the point of posting cheerful signs explaining the reason for a disruption in elevator service or why a bathroom was being repaired. "We knew customers would ask about the problem, so we told them how our construction was reinforcing our brand—that we were anticipating their needs. Answering their questions before they had to ask is part of our patient promise," said Rose.

Encouraging such self-examination also broke down the rigid hierarchy of power and made it clear that the hospital's new focus on patient care had to evolve at all levels. CEO Berrett even included his own personal telephone number in the new Patient and Family Guide, and encouraged patients to call with concerns. "He wasn't bombarded. It didn't take over his life. But when people did dial it, they were stunned to find it actually rang to his phone," said Rose.

As employees saw their leaders and colleagues making real, personal changes in their approach to patient care, new kinds of relationships began to develop within Medical City. Something about seeing real change happen around them helped employees to trust each other and impacted even the most entrenched teams.

The Posse realized it was time to shift gears again. With an Orange Revolution in full motion at Medical City, the team again held up the mirror, but this time to recognize employee achievements. "We celebrate every chance we get," said Rose, explaining that when the hospital recently achieved a whooping 3.7 customer-satisfaction rating, they celebrated with a Patient Pizza Promise, delivering more than five hundred pies to all shifts.

Looking at Medical City today, it's hard to believe that it once was off course. Employee turnover has fallen from 36 percent to 6. And it is now one of the top-rated hospitals in parent company HCA's system of 160 hospitals (often ranking in first place).

The most remarkable part of the entire transformation, said Rose, is that most of the changes originated—and continue to originate—from individual employees and teams. "As leadership, we communicate, communicate, communicate the need. But we depend on employees to come up with the ideas and implement the behaviors necessary to reach our common cause, our patient promise," said Rose.

Medical City's Posse members aren't alone in their commitment to communicating the cause. Articulating a shared vision clearly, consistently, and emphatically is crucial to any successful change initiative. Still, some people believe that a common vision must be of major social significance before people will rally behind it—eradicating poverty, for instance. But the reality is far simpler. People want clear meaning in their jobs. Our global research with Towers Watson in 2008 discovered the third most important predictor of employee engagement was having pride in your organization, especially in the manifestation of its symbol, and the number one driver of that pride was "alignment." In other words, as an employee you stand a much greater chance of being engaged if you believe your organization is aligned to what it stands for: whether amazing customer service, cutting-edge innovation, or out-of-this-world patient care.

This usually involves taking the cause beyond numbers. Medical City, for example, could have communicated a quantifiable goal of increasing customer satisfaction to 3.7 out of 4, but that would not have resonated with employees the way the challenge did to make raving fans out of their patients.

In the National Basketball Association's marketing team, which you'll read about in chapter 4, their cause was to reaffirm the NBA's status as the world's preeminent sports league. The result was all-time records in attendance. For the Madison Square Garden Sports team, their new cause is to create what they call Forever Memories for every one of their guests. In a division of food distributor Nash Finch, which supports military families, their cause is to treat their customers like heroes. As a result, they've developed creative ways to ensure military families living on bases around the world can still find the comforts of home, because that's how you treat heroes.

Causes are the driving forces of the teams we studied. And yet, in the process of articulating a cause and gaining full buy-in, these groups have encountered their share of land mines. The first is the tendency for complexity. While a cause is a single purpose that defines what we are all about, too many of us have worked in teams with so many priorities that it's hard to keep them straight in our heads, let alone reach an agreement on which overriding idea will guide everything we do.

And even if a team achieves agreement on a single cause, other hurdles emerge; for instance, employee resistance. Fear of the unknown, comfort with the status quo, or even personal agendas can cause people to determinedly cling to what's known, despite indicators that point to bumpy roads ahead. Cynicism can also run rampant when teams are seeking buy-in. Many of us have worked at places where the commitment to a professed cause was hardly aligned with actions. And because of that we learned to keep our heads down and wait out new change initiatives. It is essential that employees feel leaders are authentic about their commitment to the cause before they buy in.

But as challenging as the work of articulating, agreeing on, and getting buy-in to a cause may seem, the alternative is unacceptable for teams seeking to break out. Without a clear, larger purpose, setting the standard for how the team should be operating and what priorities should exist, teams can become blown off course easily, lose focus, or even become dominated by strong personalities (alienating everyone from a sense of ownership). Our team learned this lesson the hard way a few years ago.

Here's what happened. Early in the development of our business books we experienced a surge of interest in our training offerings. Our speaking and workshop business tripled in just one year. With such growth came challenges. We debated how to structure ourselves, where to focus people and budget, and how we could best continue to grow and spread the message.

To help organize ourselves as a real business division, and to allow us to focus the majority of our time serving clients and continuing to publish, we brought in a senior leader to head up the business side of the enterprise. We assumed that meant standardized billing, finding us more resources, and reminding us of our P&L once a month.

The executive had other ideas. Within weeks of coming in, with little idea about our business or the training world in general, and having spoken to no one on the team, he saw the indecisiveness inherent in the growing operation and became what Bob Frisch, managing partner of the Strategic Offsites Group in Boston, calls "dictator by default."

He began making big decisions by himself, announcing that he would bring in new managers (over our loyal people), remove team members (who had worked for us for years), and integrate our team into another unrelated area of our parent company. One morning at a breakfast meeting, he informed us of his plan and nixed any further discussion. One of us remembers wondering what prison sentence we would have to serve if we stuck the sharp end of a fork in the man's eye.

Much too late, we realized our core mistake. We had brought this partner into our pursuit without clearly articulating our shared cause, perhaps because we had not been fully aware of it ourselves at the time. It was only when we were faced with such a stark contrast that we finally understood that building the business was not our cause, but just a way to accomplish our raison d'être. Our cause was to become a manager's best friend—providing the tools managers needed to build stronger teams. And we knew that we didn't want to do it alone. We wanted to do it with our team. We realized we valued being an innovative, entrepreneurial enterprise within a larger organization.

Up until this leader joined us, roles had been changing and evolving as needed, not under a hierarchical command-and-control structure, but under an Orange team model where we all felt equal responsibility for the group's success or failure. We began to understand the incredible value of what we had. Suddenly, we knew that working with one another for the good of the cause was, in fact, central to our cause.

What followed was a very difficult year spent trying to reach a level of cooperation with this executive. Eventually we parted ways with him and achieved autonomy again, this time with an enhanced understanding of and appreciation for our shared cause.

At Zappos.com, CEO Tony Hsieh anticipated this type of identify crisis before it happened.

THE CAUSE TO WOW

Indeed, at the world's most remarkable online shoe retailer, we found one of the world's most unique company mission statements: "to live and deliver wow." Zappos' succinct and wacky cause is largely due to the work of Hsieh. Like other revolutionary team leaders, he is convinced that it's the clarity of the Zappos mission that drives its unique culture and stacks the competitive deck in their favor.

Now, if you've shopped Zappos.com you know they have a great product strategy—allowing you to shop for shoes and other stuff with free shipping both ways. So, in effect, you can try on a pair of Hush Puppies and never leave home. But, as good as those ideas are, they could be replicated. "They [the competition] can copy the look and feel of our website and even, eventually, the brands we have signed up. What they can't copy is our culture. That's our competitive advantage," Hsieh told us.

The balance sheet seems to indicate that this CEO knows what he is talking about. Despite being only ten years old, this online retailer reports annual sales in excess of $1.1 billion.

We've never seen an environment like this. As you tour the Las Vegas complex (wearing your mandatory crown and stopping to have your picture taken on a throne) you quickly note that Zappos employees want to wow in every interaction with each other and their customers. Where to begin to explain? There's the fashion department that shows visitors how important they are by taking their pictures (pretending they are paparazzi), or how about the finance team (yes, those fun and crazy accountants) who are cleaning up from their soap box car race. They believe part of wowing each other is having fun as a group. There's a counseling area, where employees meet with coach Dr. David Vik to set personal wow goals—everything from losing weight, to getting out of debt, to getting promoted. Even the parking lot had been the site of an event the day before, an attempt by HR to wow all the employees by letting them cuddle a rabbit. We could go on and on.

If you think that's weird, you're right. Being a little "weird" is actually one of the ten ways employees live their mission. These ten core values include ideas such as being "adventurous, creative, and open-minded," having a "family spirit," and even being "humble." When we speak with Maura Sullivan, customer loyalty manager, she can't wait to list the values for us, which she does by heart, with no advance warning.

"Wow, ten, just like Moses," we say, impressed.

"They're written on a stone tablet somewhere around here," chimes in Rob Siefker, senior manager of customer loyalty.

Employees spent a year helping to determine the ten, all culled from a list of thirty-seven concepts provided by Hsieh.

"Create Fun and a Little Weirdness" has definitely become a favorite, says Christa Foley, the company's recruiting manager. "For us, it's about being creative and being out of the box and taking risks. It kind of incorporates a whole bunch of core values into one; and for us weird is a very positive thing, where normal might be the negative."

While ten rules might seem overwhelming for employees to get their heads around, at Zappos there is great clarity about them, because the company takes the time to communicate these values over and over, from the temporary tattoo parlor in the front hall allowing you to decorate your body with your favorite value, to cafeteria team sing-offs that reinforce the ten in amusing song parodies. It's all so weirdly wonderful that's it's a little hard to take in.

Sullivan reminds us that this devotion to the cause of Wow, with the ten values to help everyone get there, builds a foundational level of trust at Zappos that gives employees the room to translate wow into their daily actions.

"People ask, 'What's your secret to giving Wow service?' It's really about putting trust and empowerment in our reps to make decisions right on the spot," she said. "Whether it's shipping out a free pair of shoes, giving a coupon, setting up a UPS pickup . . . they don't need to ask a supervisor, they are more than welcome to go ahead and do it and not feel restricted with all kinds of policies."

Rebecca Ratner, director of HR, couldn't agree more. "When I came on board two years ago, even at the more senior level, it was a huge chance to walk in and make decisions I thought were right for the department or for the company and not have seventeen levels of approvals to go through. Here it's important to be yourself, live the values, do right by the company, and do right by what you believe in." In the background, we hear a burst of music by the Red Hot Chili Peppers and an impromptu parade begins. More weirdness. More fun. More Wow.

Hsieh admits that keeping Zappos focused on this cause through the against-the-grain culture isn't easy; they have to work on it constantly. But there's a method to the madness: The intent of all this Wow "is to do something that's above-and-beyond what's expected, something that has an emotional impact on the receiver."

It seems to be working, just as it is in breakthrough teams all around the world. Over the next few chapters, we'll introduce you to some amazing groups that are passionate about their causes. Their purposes may seem as different as night and day, and yet they do share some similarities. Breakthrough teams establish transformational common causes in several ways:

1. They involve employees at all levels in establishing not only the cause, but the values to get there.
2. They align the team cause with the larger goals of the organization.
3. They create a unique, concise cause statement that helps make the team stand out in its industry.
4. They communicate the shared purpose clearly and frequently, holding it up like a rallying flag.
5. They align goals, deadlines, and celebrations to the cause.

As you'll find, it's remarkable how powerful a single common rallying point can be in establishing breakthrough results. In fact, the path to turning your team Orange starts with a clear cause.

3

Competence: Back to the Basics (+ Recognition)

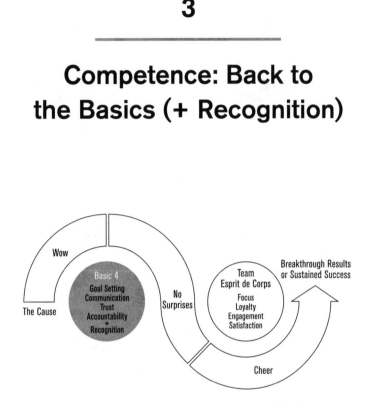

Imagine it's a quarter past the dawn of time and early man is out hunting. The fellow (perhaps accompanied by an equally hungry relative) spots a woolly mammoth. A tussle ensues; a dozen spears are launched at the huge, menacing animal. Finally after exhausting all but the last javelin, our hero places its point between two of the mammoth's ribs, piercing the heart. Lucky early man is able to take the meat home to roast on the cave fire.

That image, for years propagated by anthropologists, has been replaced with a different vision. Most likely our ancient ancestors were no more able to wrestle to the ground a huge beast than we are; but they did excel at running. It appears that we are evolutionarily predisposed to run long distances.

The new theory is that a team of early men had to work together. Personal competencies were maximized for the good of the group. Those with heightened tracking skills spotted the spore or prints. Others with leadership abilities positioned the men to surprise the animal in an advantageous location. Those with the most accurate arms would wound a beast with their spears and scare it into a run, while the rest of the team would take up the chase—pursuing the animal for hours or even days until it dropped of exhaustion. The hunt took much more teamwork, over a longer period of time, than we had ever imagined.

That's a protracted way of saying that as a species, we're team people. We live in communities for a reason. We developed skills to communicate, safeguard, and find happiness in groups. Given a range of skills needed to survive (without natural protection of thick skin, warm coats, intense sprinting ability, or strength for our size), we band together to compensate for each other's deficiencies and to magnify our singular abilities.

But if people come to the idea of teams so naturally, why are there so many bad teams and why are organizations in general so bad at teamwork? Why do we have an entire generation of people struggling to figure out how to work together?

In short, because we are also bred to exhibit very unteamlike behavior.

It would be easy to lay blame here on those who can't get along and work collaboratively, but the hard facts are that there really are a hundred reasons *not* to bond with our co-workers. Top among them is our natural tendency to compete at the expense of others. According to an Office Team survey of senior executives, nearly half said they believe employees are "more competitive" with each other than a decade ago. And an additional 12 percent described the rivalry as "significantly more competitive."

This inbred enmity became increasingly clear to us while meeting with one sales organization. Turnover among the senior sales staff was virtually nonexistent, while more than half of the junior sales group quit annually. The reasons weren't hard to fathom. As we talked with senior team members, they admitted that compensation and reward systems encouraged them to hoard leads and compete directly with their up-and-coming talent, hire only underwhelming subordinates who would pose no threat to their jobs, and even blame their associates if they lost a deal. All of this created an environment of increasing risk for the company—an aging senior staff with very few qualified individuals to replace older workers as they retired.

Employees in this organization were obviously lacking in the first quality that we found in abundance in breakthrough teams—a heightened sense of esprit de corps and the tendency to value team members above others. But there was something more.

Great teams have an expectation of personal competence: they hire for it, they nurture it. This sales organization did everything possible to undermine personal competency in the junior members of their staff. It's one illustration of how conflicted we are as organizations and as human beings: We understand the innate importance of working together, but our cultural competitive natures, not to mention our negatively designed corporate structures, can pull us apart.

So how on earth do you as a team leader, team member, or senior executive get people to buck the insidious forces that can make our teams dysfunctional?

The answer will take us deep into our research over the rest of this chapter to identify the Orange characteristics that promote personal competency and allow a group of qualified individuals to band together to create a breakthrough team. We're hoping, as you read through the pages, that you will experience a bit of an aha moment. After all, most of us assume that success in business comes from making our numbers or meeting our quotas, performing our duties well, showing up on time and staying late, and so on. Those are important ingredients, but they are just part of the story.

PERSONAL COMPETENCE

With high unemployment and fierce competition for good jobs in the current economy, we might assume that personal competency would be a given among today's workers. Yet it's estimated that worker incompetence and mistakes cost businesses up to 25 percent of their revenue each year. And while a comedy of errors may make for great theater, in business employee error hurts us all, especially in mistrust. After all, we don't often pass to a teammate we think will bobble the ball; we wouldn't assign a solo to a musician we don't believe could hit the notes. Most of us will go to great lengths to avoid collaborating with a co-worker who has a reputation for shoddy work. It is ludicrous to expect team members to value co-workers they don't respect. It would be equally impossible for those same team members to achieve transformational results without the requisite skill sets.

It follows, then, that to achieve breakthrough results, each team member must first establish a level of personal competency. After all, the extra effort involved in rerouting around the weak links of our groups slows productivity and reduces the time we can devote to the projects that create the largest impact. Within any organization, at least 80 percent of our days are spent maintaining the status quo. It's the additional 20 percent, the above-and-beyond efforts, that move us forward. If our spare time is monopolized by repairing errors rather than doing what matters most, it is impossible to move ahead.

That's one reason breakthrough teams place such a high value on competence, protecting their above-and-beyond time by demanding openness if someone is struggling or needs clarification about a goal or specific need; trusting that their colleagues will seek out the information and expertise they need from each other; enhancing their skills with training inside or outside the company. And of course they hold each other to a high standard of performance.

By creating an Orange culture that not only expects but also nurtures competency, and then combining it with a high regard for team members, breakthrough teams generate a self-perpetuating collaborative energy.

We have seen this often in highly functioning health care organizations. Researchers at one hospital surveyed nurses in such an environment to find out which co-workers they consulted when confronted with complex treatment situations. The nurses were much more likely to seek consults from co-workers they believed had relevant experience (those who were competent), who they viewed as accessible (who were willing to share information and expertise), and with whom they had a trusting relationship (those who had a high regard for fellow team members).

Personal expertise, an open environment, and team respect allowed these medical professionals to seek the help they needed more readily, discuss issues more honestly, and pool their talents to solve problems. All of which saved lives.

Managers play a vital role in ensuring such competence exists. Effective leaders not only help set the team's vision, remove obstacles, and lead celebrations, but they also play a pivotal role in bringing capable people aboard. And they handle the difficult conversations when it's clear a team member is not qualified for his or her current role. One manager in a customer service role told us that she and her team are "slow to hire," ensuring new people have the right skills and team chemistry; but she added they are "quick to fire," if they've made a mistake and a new employee can't grasp the complexities of the job or work well with others.

To identify the best and brightest, Thomas Edison created his own unique tests, ranging from asking prospective team members to conduct impromptu experiments to challenging them to assemble machine parts on the spot without instructions. Some were subjected to rigorous questioning on a broad range of general interest topics.

"What city in the United States leads in making laundry machines?" Edison asked one potential team member. "Why is cast iron called pig iron?" "Who was Solon?"

Englishman Samuel Insull was not even given time to unpack his bags before undergoing his customized examination. Arriving in New York in the evening after a rough, two-month voyage from England, and having nowhere to stay the night, he went directly to Edison's office. There, Edison wasted no time in explaining that his London agent was leaving for Europe the next day to round up cash for Edison's next project. Would Insull immediately identify which of Edison's assets could be used to generate funds?

Despite his exhaustion and surprise, Insull rose to the challenge. Taking time only to eat a quick dinner, he went to work reviewing Edison's complicated and untidy financial documents throughout the night. By morning, he and Edison had drawn up an inspired plan. He passed the test and was admitted to Edison's inner circle as a trusted personal and financial advisor.

And yet Insull's competence was hard-won. Before setting sail for the new world, he had worked as a jack-of-all-trades assistant in the UK branch of Edison's Mercantile Trust Company, where his days were filled with handling simple correspondence, filing, maintaining telephone batteries, and even operating the first switchboard for Edison's small London telephone system. His personal revolution started when Edward Johnson, Edison's chief agent in England, roared into the office one day in a frenzy. Johnson needed a stenographer to prepare a legal brief on short notice and couldn't find one. Seeing a chance to gain valuable knowledge and experience, Insull volunteered.

That brief, and the work Insull continued to do for Johnson in his spare time, gave the pale and bespectacled assistant a window of insight into Edison's contracts, financing, income, and expenditures. It also provided a valuable referral. In the end, it was Johnson who recommended Insull to Edison himself, launching Samuel Insull's trip to America and his fateful meeting with the genius.

As we traveled around the world conducting interviews for this book, we met a variety of teams that, like Insull, were paying the price to increase their worth to each other. In one IT department we visited, almost half the members were currently pursuing advanced degrees. Sam, a busy programmer with four children at home, was in his mid-forties. He explained that he was almost finished with his MBA, paying for it out of his own pocket and investing two nights a week in class. "We were sitting around at lunch one day talking. I think we'd all reached a point where we couldn't wait anymore to invest in our future; we had to take responsibility for our own personal development."

Another: Christine told us she purposely joined the marketing team at a state university when her youngest child started school full time. The pay was certainly not the draw (it was embarrassing compared with her pre-child days), but she wanted "to work with people who were constantly expanding their skill sets. I mean, we all get free tech training, free seminars. We have to do it on our own time, but it's a great place to grow."

Other teams we met encouraged each other to join professional organizations with the aim of increasing their knowledge base and network. Several teams met each month to discuss the latest business book to stay sharp.

All this is impressive. But the thing that makes it truly revolutionary is the reason they're doing it: not to outperform each other, but to become more *credible* to each other—to offer a heightened level of competence and expertise to their fellow workers.

Still, this is not a book dedicated to improving technical performance. Job proficiency is the foundation for personal competence, but is simply being good at your job what creates sustained results? This is where the research comes in to hone the key principles. Over the following pages we will introduce you to several characteristics that many business people view as "soft," ideas such as recognition, goal setting, trust, and so on. While these concepts may seem fluffy, we will show that they actually drive competence every bit as much as technical ability.

And the correlation to our study of teams? These so-called soft characteristics are those found in the members of breakthrough teams.

The more adept you become at these traits, the more engaged you will become on the job and the more competent you will be viewed by colleagues and bosses. And when the vast majority of people on your team embrace these traits, the better your collective results are. It's that simple.

The bottom line is that we can't fake our way to breakthrough results. They come at a cost; and the price of breakthrough teamwork is actually a personal journey that starts with each member of the group.

THE BASIC 4+ RECOGNITION

We've been studying the characteristics of the best managers for almost twenty years. In our ten-year research study for *The Carrot Principle*, we discovered that leaders who achieve enhanced business results are significantly more apt to be seen by their employees as stronger in the following areas (what we called the Basic 4 + Recognition):

- Goal setting (knowing where you are going)
- Communication (wise use of your voice and ears)
- Trust (believing in others and being trustworthy)
- Accountability (doing what you say you will do)

Plus

- Recognition (appreciating others' strengths)

The impact of these characteristics on the bottom line was irrefutable. When leaders combined these Basic 4 leadership characteristics (as we called them) with frequent, purpose-based recognition, return on equity was more than three times higher than returns experienced by leaders who didn't display these qualities, and team morale more than twice as high. In addition, the teams and offices rated most highly by employees for the Basic 4 + Recognition also typically place in the top scores for customer satisfaction, employee satisfaction, and retention.

All these are admirable outcomes showing that simply being good at your work won't cut it. As a manager, you need to offer your teammates a good deal on the so-called "soft" side of the ledger.

Still, even for leaders who bought into the need to nurture, it was hard to believe that these traits could have that kind of impact; mostly because the characteristics are not flashy. They are so fundamental, in fact, that most of us have skipped over them in our quest to achieve transformational results. We've been so focused on finding something bigger, new, or startling to transform our workplaces, that we've ignored familiar and less glamorous characteristics like trust and communication. The irony is that while they suffer from the "girl-next-door" syndrome, the Basic 4 + Recognition are a vital part of a manager's personal competency and exactly what is needed to succeed.

For Brice Fukumoto, however, it was love at first sight. He recognized the importance of these simple traits from the minute he was exposed to them.

We met with Fukumoto in 2008 when he was general manager of one of the terminals at Newark Airport in New Jersey. We were enjoying a pleasant visit together when he confided, "I've read your book *The Carrot Principle*. I've dog-eared the pages and highlighted here and there. I believe you." We thanked him for the support, but he shook his head. That wasn't the point; he had a challenge for us.

He motioned to the sprawling operation that was his daily routine. He managed 150 employees who oversaw six gates and eighteen flights daily to points around the globe. The team members were busy boarding flights, answering passenger questions, loading baggage, making repairs, cleaning and fueling planes. It was a beehive of activity.

"I'm just one guy," he said. "Wouldn't it be better if you got everyone here to buy in?"

Fukumoto's challenge—in essence *how do I get everyone involved?*—became repeated over and over during this work. Could individual team members buy in to the Basic 4 + Recognition to enhance their effectiveness? And if so, was there something after that? How could a team of such personally competent individuals band together to create breakthrough results?

With those questions circling, at the end of 2009 we enlisted the help of an independent research firm. Our first task was to validate if the attributes of the Basic 4 + Recognition were indeed part of the personal competencies needed to start an Orange Revolution. Next, we asked for statistical insights into the role team affiliation plays in creating a great workplace and inspiring regular people to become great players.

The research was culled from the 350,000-person database of Harrisburg, Pennsylvania–based Best Companies Group (BCG), which works with partners throughout the United States and Canada to establish "Best Places to Work" programs. You've probably seen one of these "Best" lists in a newspaper, magazine, or on television in New York, California, Texas, Florida, or numerous other states and provinces. They also conduct national "Best" programs in health care, insurance, accounting, law, marketing, media, and other industries. BCG's goal is to recognize companies in a geographic area or industry that have been successful in creating what they call "workplace excellence." These workplaces enjoy higher levels of employee engagement, which has been shown to increase employee morale, produce higher quality applicants, enhance recruiting efforts, and even elevate profitability and shareholder returns.

Their data provides rock solid statistical validity to the ideas we'll present in *The Orange Revolution*.

BCG analyzed its database of more than 350,000 people: 117,000 were interviewed in 2008 and 240,000 in 2009. Employees from twenty-eight industries were studied—from accounting to government, health care to technology, financial services to education, services to manufacturing.

With such great data at our fingertips, we felt certain BCG could provide a definitive answer to these growing questions:

- Do the Basic 4 + Recognition truly enhance the concept of personal competency and employee engagement?
- What are the differences between companies that make a Best Places to Work list versus those that do not? And what are some insights around teamwork that might help good companies become great?

What became clear with our new research is that the Basic 4 + Recognition aren't the exclusive realm of management. They are also traits shared by *members*, not just leaders, of breakthrough teams. It was a significant learning experience for us: individual contributors who live these basics of leadership are vastly more engaged in their work and deliver superior results. When enough members of your team exhibit these qualities, great things happen collectively. And as you can imagine, when the majority of your team don't, you experience average or poor results, dysfunctional relationships, and turnover.

To conduct a deep analysis, we asked BCG to identify what created "engaged" teammates—people who were fully invested in their work and their team. To make this classification, as part of a Best Places to Work list, BCG asks dozens of questions that measure employee opinions on all aspects of the work experience, from leadership to planning to team camaraderie to work environment to pay and benefits. In particular, BCG has found that five response areas are most likely to indicate an employee is feeling engaged on his or her team:

- Overall employee satisfaction
- Likelihood of employee to recommend employment to a friend
- Likelihood of employee to recommend the company's products and services
- Likelihood of employee to remain employed at least two more years
- Willingness of employee to give extra effort when asked

Employees who agree or strongly agree to questions relating to the five ideas above are considered engaged and feel they are part of a great team. These employees work in groups or departments that are willing to take ownership of problems; provide innovation and ideas; have a desire to contribute to the success of their organization; and have an emotional bond to the company, its mission, and vision.

But then we wanted to know what was different about these engaged employees. Would they be more inclined to set clear goals, would they feel more open communication was happening, would they feel more recognized? Our first task was to identify what we called (for simplicity) the Orange Revolution questions, ten queries from the BCG survey that our hypothesis predicted would enhance personal competency. If our theory was right, on teams that were engaged, the vast majority of employees would answer these ten questions (detailed in the appendix) positively. And, in turn, we expected that employees on disengaged teams would answer the ten negatively.

We had no idea of the magnitude of the difference the researchers would discover.

We see in the data below that employees become more engaged as they believe their teams, leaders, and organizations set clear goals, communicate openly, build trust, hold them accountable, and recognize great work. Only 4 percent of employees feel part of an engaging team environment when they report not one of their Basic 4 + Recognition

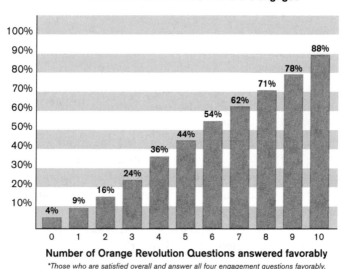

Percent of team members who are engaged*

Number of Orange Revolution Questions answered favorably

Those who are satisfied overall and answer all four engagement questions favorably.

needs being met, however 88 percent are engaged when they answer all ten key questions favorably. In other words, in a team that incorporates the Basic 4 + Recognition, almost nine out of ten employees are fully engaged: the first step toward revolutionary results. Try to play on a team without these Orange Revolution essentials, and less than one in twenty people will play with you.

Next we asked the researchers to cut the data so we could identify any differences on the Basic 4 + Recognition scores between organizations that made a Best Places to Work list and those good firms that wanted to be included but missed the cut. It's important to remember that these are all very solid organizations, companies that truly believed they were strong enough to receive the acclaim of being on a "Best Places to Work" list.

What arose from the data were several interesting statistical variances related to these issues. In considering where to improve, teams and organizations should consider strengthening the following aspects of their work experience:

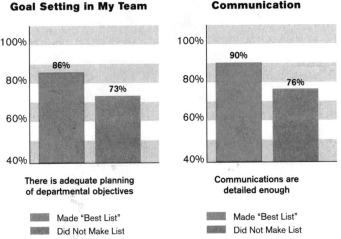

Goal Setting in My Team

86%
73%

There is adequate planning
of departmental objectives

▇ Made "Best List"
▇ Did Not Make List

Communication

90%
76%

Communications are
detailed enough

▇ Made "Best List"
▇ Did Not Make List

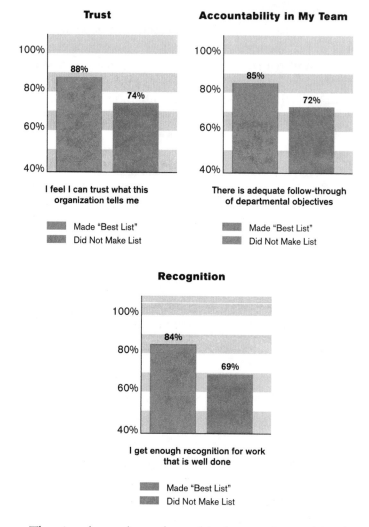

Trust

I feel I can trust what this organization tells me

Made "Best List"
Did Not Make List

Accountability in My Team

There is adequate follow-through of departmental objectives

Made "Best List"
Did Not Make List

Recognition

I get enough recognition for work that is well done

Made "Best List"
Did Not Make List

There's a lot to learn from this data, and one thing is absolutely clear: in the best companies the Basic 4 + Recognition traits are practiced deep in the organization. So, if we're going to focus on developing personal competency, then goal setting, communication, trust, accountability, and recognition should command our first and finest efforts. In fact, that last graph on recognition is telling. There is a 15 point swing in recognition scores between organizations that made the list and those that did not—the largest delta on the questions we measured. That variation is not only classified by researchers as statistically significant, but indicates that we should put much more emphasis on cheering for each other through recognition and appreciation.

It's one final number of many that provide a powerful statistical foundation to build on. But before we get ahead of ourselves, let's focus on goal setting. It's a natural starting point for our discussion, since it's hard to succeed at anything without a clear direction.

GOAL SETTING

Wouldn't it be nirvana if pursuing the activities of most benefit to your team tapped your greatest strengths and were personally rewarding? And yet for breakthrough team members, a greater percentage of their activities are just that.

In our interviews with members of top-performing teams, we found that they regularly take the time to identify goals that align with their personal competencies as well as with team, company, and customer needs. By doing so, they ensure that not only will their efforts have personal meaning, but they'll have impact on the world around them.

They begin the process of identifying these mutually beneficial goals by asking themselves, "What can I be world class at?" Having defined a place where they can add the most value, they compare each goal against team and company objectives by asking questions like these:

- Does this goal play to our team strengths? (And can we realistically accomplish it?)
- Does it benefit our team, customers, or company? (Does it support what matters most around here?)

- Is it ethical? (It's okay to take a risk, but could it possibly get us in trouble?)
- Are we accountable for a result? (Do we have a deadline and promised deliverable?)
- Is it in line with our team or company values? (Would we be proud if our goal was written up on the front page of the company newsletter?)

We have observed that after undergoing this process, individuals and teams often discover that the activities which have the most impact and are most fulfilling are not part of their defined daily tasks. That's not a bad thing; in fact, it's desirable to stretch, because the discrepancy prompts ongoing discussions of team priorities and individual roles, further sharpening a breakthrough team's focus on shared goals. If you consider how rarely group goals are on the radar of employees within traditional teams, the value of such discussions is instantly clear, begging the question: what can we achieve at a world-class level?

The ancient Greeks understood the importance of aligning your personal competencies with team goals. They called the ability to give your best in the area where you have the best to give *eudaimonia*. A University of Alberta study proved the concept in modern times. The Canadian researchers involved two groups of health care workers. One group of randomly selected staff members attended a workshop followed by eight weekly hour-long follow-up sessions where they participated in exercises designed to help them set clear goals that would focus them on work that both had value to others *and* would excite and satisfy them. In other words, they were given time to pursue eudaimonia. The second group was a control group. They went about their work lives as usual.

Both groups were asked to fill out detailed questionnaires before the workshop and five months after. Not surprisingly, the group that didn't participate in the exercises saw no measurable change in engagement with their work. However, the eudaimonia group experienced a 10 percent increase in job satisfaction and a 17 percent rise in workplace morale. In addition, absenteeism was cut by more than half, from 4 percent a month to 1.7 percent.

That's the power of Orange at work.

Judd Garcia Tecson's team is a prime example. We met this remarkable group of employees while staying at the Pan Pacific Hotel in Singapore. Tecson and his colleagues had found their Orange core. We interviewed Tecson while he answered a steady stream of cell phone calls from his teammates who were asking questions. We noted that his drivers were clear: he and his team were motivated first by a desire to create unique experiences for their guests, second by the autonomy and trust they were offered, and finally by the daily recognition offered by their fellow teammates and superiors.

"Every day I come to work is a miracle. We each make our own decisions about how to best serve our guests. That creativity is very important."

The goal from corporate is simple yet provides a tremendous amount of liberty to team members: "Do what is good for the company and what is good for guests." No matter the cost, no matter the trouble it takes.

"Yesterday, we set up a trail of rose petals for a couple that is celebrating their thirty-second wedding anniversary. We put white and red rose petals heading all the way to the bedroom. I put some candles in the room, cakes, champagne. The sky is the limit of what we can do for guests, as long as we remember our commitment to be accountable and responsible with decisions. Each of us feels like the general manager in our department."

That closing statement from Tecson is most telling. Each member of his team feels like the GM. And, as we interviewed the team members, it was amazing to see how every single person knew, understood, and focused on that same goal. Their team goal (creativity) is in line with their personal goal (autonomy) and their company goal (out of this world service), and that alignment brings exceptional results every day. In fact, when we returned a few months after this interview, Tecson was working with a new team in a newly expanded role. He had just been promoted to run the hotel's exclusive Pacific Club.

What happens when individual goals and team goals don't align? Demise is swift. Basically, teams will separate; there is little to keep them together. When clear goals aren't understood by all team members, dysfunction ensues. And we've heard the result time and again. Typically the stories begin with, "Ha, that's nothing! At my last job . . ."

As a practical point, it's actually hard to set just one goal; setting two is easier. When you establish both a quantified goal and a behavioral goal at the same time, they work hand in hand to propel you forward. For example, a salesperson might set a quantifiable goal to sell so many units of a product in the first quarter. The quantifiable goal contains a desired result in number and completion date. A behavioral goal might be to make fourteen prospecting calls or research three new companies each week. The behavioral goal outlines the way you will reach the quantifiable goal. Alone, the quantifiable objective might be overwhelming; but the behavioral goal breaks it down into manageable activities.

Of course, as you work toward your goal, don't neglect to set aside time on a regular basis to evaluate your progress. Done this way, the goal-setting formula looks much like directions for a trip: You set a destination, chart a way there, evaluate progress along the way, and repeat as needed.

COMMUNICATION

Open communication enhances business success, making everything faster, better. It's a staple of great teams. But why? It's important to note that communication is not only made up of messages sent, but also messages received. In other words, if people don't comprehend the messages they get from co-workers or managers, communication fails, goals are missed, trust is shattered. Breakthrough teams understand this—members realize that listening is as important as talking. Frequency of communication is as important as specificity and timeliness.

But what should be commonly practiced is rare and unpredictable.

One CEO we sat down with, during our focus group discussions and interviews, used the terms "candor," "freedom to disagree," and "I've got your back," as he described his working team as it exists today. But this tight-knit group of senior executives wasn't always so close. After early tension and political infighting, they had to *learn* to break down walls and communicate effectively and openly. It wasn't a natural tendency—even though most of us think we're quite good communicators.

And yet when communication is open, honest, and clear to all parties, it helps us to understand each other's motivations and intents. It can establish where we are, where we want to go, and how to get there. It can even reduce redundancy and conflict. Silence may be golden, but it doesn't contribute much to team success. And, in fact, silence says a lot. We just don't know how it's being interpreted.

The silent treatment is nonexistent within breakthrough teams. In our research and interviews, we've observed that breakthrough team members are active, if not perfect, communicators.

- They identify problems, bringing them up with the team and bosses, always with at least one potential solution.
- They share ideas freely with their colleagues.
- They pass on useful bits of information to co-workers.
- They take time to listen to team member ideas and concerns.

- They are careful in what they will promise, because they will do whatever is necessary to meet a deadline or live up to a commitment.
- They admit mistakes immediately and do whatever they can to repair the damage.
- They respond promptly to team member requests for information.
- They are the first to share credit with everyone involved.
- They recognize others' achievements publicly and proudly.
- They let others know their short- and long-term goals for future performance.

Take a moment to review that list. Are there areas where you and your team might be falling short? One of the constants we heard in our interviews with average or poor teams was this: "We don't get enough communication." Ironically we even heard this during a visit with a consulting firm that insisted upon "all-hands" stand-ups three times a week, and where the senior-most executive sent out a podcast every Monday morning to fill employees in on the latest. The point is: it's rare to meet team members who think they are getting too much communication; it's hard to get too much of this good thing.

TRUST

Of the Basic 4, the most difficult to adopt and grasp is the idea of trust. However, on breakthrough teams, trust is as critical to success as proficiency is to function. And although it may be the most elusive as you devise a plan of implementation, it can be a springboard from marginal to breakout performance. In fact, enhanced trust catapults a team almost immediately. The problem is that most people—employees and managers—believe that their co-workers already trust them. The truth, though, is that real, productive trust is a rarity in most work environments. Unlike goal setting and accountability, which seem even to the most cynical as inevitable in fostering greater effort from those around us, trust involves accepting a bit of blame now and then—counterintuitive in the traditional "the buck-stops-anywhere-but-here" work environment. It also involves letting go of control and placing greater faith in your colleagues.

Despite extensive lip service about diversity, most of us inherently distrust workers who are different from us. While we easily accept that a dolphin will never fly, a kangaroo will never climb a tree, and a cheetah will never win a swimming race, we cannot make the same leap of logic concerning our co-workers. We can't understand why Jan can't be more analytical, like us. Why Eric isn't more diplomatic. Rather than appreciate their strengths, each a key to our survival as a team, we view their uniqueness as flaws or liabilities.

It shouldn't be surprising, then, that in our research we found pockets of resentment by co-workers toward the individuality and distinct qualities of their peers. And in turn, many co-workers undermine the reputations of their teammates, significantly reducing trust and camaraderie.

We saw this exemplified in a southeastern financial industry firm, where an HR staff member had surprisingly become a local media darling. All it took was one interview, where she provided insight on growing start-ups, for the camera to fall in love with her and her engaging personality. She was funny and genuine, and provided memorable sound bites. Within weeks she had been asked to provide comments to several local television stations, the newspaper, and a few blogs, providing free publicity for her company with every mention.

But rather than inspire cheers at work, her popularity began to engender jealousy among peers and higher-ups, who complained that an HR staffer was not the appropriate source for such commentary. In response, the firm issued a memo that required a particular senior vice president to respond to all press inquiries. The man was certainly knowledgeable, but proved to be as hard to get a hold of as Batman and about as interesting as a visit to the orthodontist. The media inquiries quickly died off, and with it, the free publicity.

Was this a situation of jealousy or one of mistrust? Both emotions played into the final decision; however, it is clear that the organization suffered a loss by suspecting not only this HR staffer's abilities, but her intent. The press was amplifying the woman's voice, and that was increasing her power. If her peers and superiors could have trusted her, imagine how much publicity the company could have enjoyed.

When we decide that it isn't possible to achieve anything positive within our current team, and dismiss unique co-worker contributions, we send the message that we don't believe in their abilities, or worse, their intentions; and trust and communication are damaged. Slowly, our colleagues begin to resist sharing ideas and talents. Eventually, we find ourselves in a room full of people working separately. It's a shame, but our negative assessment of our co-workers has created a self-fulfilling prophesy: nothing good happens precisely because we don't let it.

In society, there is a heavy consequence for a lack of trust. Paul Zak, professor of economics at Claremont University, found that when less than 30 percent of people trust each other, poverty typically increases. At work, the impact of a lack of trust is just as stark; we experience a dearth of ideas and solutions dry up.

To avoid this, one fellow we interviewed in a large Atlanta advertising agency created his own mantra for dealing with co-workers with divergent talents and viewpoints in an Orange way. He said, "I remind myself that if

I shut everyone else out, then I only get the best of me on a project. But if I let everyone else in, I get the best of everyone. That's always far and away much better than I could have done on my own."

Mark Eggerding, senior vice president of street sales for U.S. Foodservice, a 29,000-person company, has adopted a similar approach. He explained, "In a team, you need some people who are thinkers, some doers, some go-getters, some people who worry about other people, some creative people. You need a blend of all types of talents and disciplines."

Eggerding's point is not about just about team member selection—although that's how most great teams are built. It's also about all members trusting one another to do their fair share of the lifting, but in their own unique ways.

In our discovery, we found team members who embraced a similar ethos did a few things right:

- They asked for input and assistance from co-workers.
- They gave help as requested, even when a job was outside their duties.
- They let their hair down occasionally, becoming vulnerable.
- They compromised when it was necessary.
- They took ownership of their mistakes.
- They took thoughtful risks.
- They refrained from talking about absent team members.
- They responded promptly to team member requests for more information.
- They proactively shared information that might be valuable to team members.

Read that list again. It's a wonderful assortment of ideas, and hopefully prompts you to work on developing a higher level of trust both personally and within your team. As you do, remember that trust must be extended with sincerity, since each of us is genetically programmed to spot the disingenuous a mile away. According to Joe Badaracco of the Harvard School of Business, this ability harks back to the earliest days of man, when knowing who could be trusted could be the difference between living or dying. And we haven't lost that ability to distinguish the genuine from the fake.

"A lot of our mental processing is unconscious. And the types of human creatures that survived in early days had warning systems for reliability and trust that we still possess," the professor said.

Our ability to survive and thrive in business depends on building trusting relationships. Notice the difference in trust between the team of early men we noted at the start of this chapter and today's typical business department. An *adequate* level of trust can help you survive; but actually reaching a *high* level of trust can make you and your team thrive. As you work toward this goal, you'll realize that the divide between your team and the amazing teams you'll read about in the coming chapters is not that significant. Continue on this path, by believing in others and being believable, and you'll soon find you're on your way toward creating another self-fulfilling prophesy. But this time, it's a positive one: You're becoming Orange.

ACCOUNTABILITY

Quite simply, accountability means that a person, or a group of people, is responsible for an outcome—good or bad. For instance, in the great teams we studied, members own their actions and outcomes. However, this type of positive accountability is the not the definition encountered in most corporate environments. Today, too many employees feel accountability is something thrust upon them when things go wrong. In other words, "Don't worry, we'll let you know if you mess up, otherwise assume you are doing okay."

Another problem with accountability in the worst performing teams? It's typically imposed upon employees who have little to no control over their situation. This type of imposed accountability is perceived as an unwelcome external judgment or demand, and employees typically express doubt about its fairness.

In either case, accountability is resented. "When I make a mistake, I'm recognized 100 percent of the time," one disgruntled employee told us. "But when I do something right, I'm not recognized 99 percent of the time." She's got a point.

Members of breakthrough teams, in contrast, see accountability as a positive. They personally embrace equal accountability for their successes and mistakes, because they have a voice in establishing expectations, and have the ability to adjust conditions, as needed, to anticipate or correct problems.

The critical difference between imposed and voluntary accountability is something as simple as empowerment. People don't want to pin their reputations to something over which they have little or no influence. That's less a career and more wagering. Giving employees the chance to participate in the development of work processes and measurements eliminates worries about unfairness and mistreatment and encourages employees to take pride in work outcomes.

We stood in a manufacturing plant one day to hear an impassioned speech by the CEO of a company struggling to recover from a crippling system overhaul. As he wrapped up his remarks he said, "I'll tell you how we're going to save this company . . . I don't know. My power doesn't include all the ideas or all the work or all the working together that we need. My brain doesn't contain all the answers, but I'll know a good one when I hear it. And I'll recognize that person for it. Our future is in your heads collectively. Together, we can be Albert Einstein. We can be geniuses. What do you say, can we do it?"

He then started listening. And ideas started coming in.

Tentatively at first. But when he recognized the good ones in public celebrations, they started *pouring* in. And when a worker had an idea, the CEO asked that individual to be accountable for the idea's success. And the result? The factory increased production, reduced the cost to deliver goods, and began to experience double-digit growth. It was a great example of what can be accomplished when employees are voluntarily accountable.

We've often reflected that the story could have had a very different ending if rather than voluntarily assume accountability as they did, leadership and employees at the plant had instead begun to place blame on their problems, imposing unfair judgments on each other. Blame paralyzes employees into inaction; and the problem is, it's dangerously pervasive in our work environments.

One example of our unconscious dependence on blame is the marketing rep we met recently after a speaking engagement. He wrapped up his mastery of personal accountability with the statement, "I wish you could speak to my team back at the office, so they would get off the pot and make something happen." This type of finger-pointing has become so integrated into our workplace communication that most of us don't even notice we are doing it unless we actively try to eradicate it; and then we are stunned by its frequency. The method for ending the blame game seems far too simple to be of consequence.

As Michelangelo explained, "I saw the angel in the marble and carved until I set him free." In like manner, overcoming our urge to fault others requires a slow and consistent removal of the thoughts that are clouding our vision. The angel is there. We just need to clean out our mental space to see it.

A simple way to begin is by restating questions without "when" or "who." Since these words move us out of the "acting" mode and into the "waiting" mode, it's a good idea to rephrase the question and place responsibility squarely in your court. Replace the other person's or group's name with "I" and use "what" or "how" instead of "when" or "who." For instance, instead of:

> *"When is our manager going to realize that she needs to recognize our achievements?"*

Move to:

> *"I wonder what I can do to thank my co-workers for their great work?"*

"What" and "how" imply ownership and promote problem solving. They prime your mind for action. Here's another example; instead of:

> *"When will Joe ever get that bid to me?"*

Move to:

> *"How can I help move that bid along?"*

The word "they" is dangerous in business. It implies something or someone is separate from you. "They" are often the scapegoats for our failures, like the ubiquitous dog that ate the homework. The tragedy is that Jan, Eric, and others are really part of the "us" that forms our team or company. In an ironic twist of corporate karma, what hurts them hurts us eventually, too.

Eliminate placing blame for just a week and you'll find it leads to some interesting exchanges:

> *"Why wasn't it delivered on time?"*
> *"Sales sold the client on some new features and they didn't . . . um, we weren't aware of them until the deadline week. It took two weeks to build them out."*

"Why weren't you aware of them?"
*"We hadn't spoken directly with sales about this client.
We are going to get better at our communication flow
on the next project. Our team is going to own that."*

Notice how the accountability is shifted back to us. Sure, it may make us a little nervous. But for our long-term reputations and the esprit de corps of our groups, there's nothing better.

RECOGNITION

Recognition is a powerful accelerant to all of the above. And it's a divider between good teams and great teams.

But in working with hundreds of organizations over the past two decades, it has become clear to us that employees who wait for managers to recognize their contributions might wait a long, long time. In 2009 alone we surveyed more than five thousand employees and managers who attended one of our recognition training sessions. More than one half reported that it had been at least six months since they were last publicly appreciated by their bosses, and more than one third said it had been a year or longer. That's despite the fact that our study in *The Carrot Principle* revealed an increase in recognition and praise leads to lower employee turnover, higher customer loyalty and satisfaction scores, and increases in overall team productivity and profitability. And this in the face of U.S. Department of Labor statistics showing that the number one reason people leave organizations is that they don't feel appreciated.

To prevent this, members of breakthrough teams don't wait for managers to catch the vision of recognition, they do it themselves. This peer-to-peer recognition is extraordinarily powerful since it comes from the people who are most respected—fellow team members—and it doesn't require a large investment of time or resources. The esprit de corps on breakthrough teams heightens the importance of genuine praise and assures recognition ceremonies have impact. In the majority of cases, this peer-to-peer appreciation takes the form of simple praise and is informal, meaning it costs little or nothing. It can be as simple as publicly giving credit where it's due, writing a thank-you note, or sending an email.

One team we met was inspired by a four-foot-tall bowling trophy that had sat neglected in the copy room for years. They decided to use the trophy as their own traveling award. The rules were simple: Whoever received the award would keep it for a few days and then pass it on to a co-worker who demonstrated a value that moved the team closer to their goals.

The trophy was large enough to take up most of a person's desk. And it was spray-painted orange, so few people passed without a comment or wisecrack. But each person in turn took pride in displaying the symbol of peer recognition (not a single one hid the trophy under their desk). And in turn each team member learned a lot about where they were going and what it took to get there.

The key for managers is to not only allow this type of peer-to-peer recognition, but encourage it and add to it with awards of their own. An interesting twist happens, however, when managers recuse themselves from the process, claiming they are too busy. While tighter bonds are formed with team members, the manager is excluded. He becomes less and less a part of the team, and less a part of the motivation equation.

Great managers have realized recognition is a key to focusing people on goals and building group cohesion. But by removing themselves from this process, some managers encourage the natural separation between leaders and subordinates. Teams can become disgruntled with their leadership—actually attempting to outperform their bosses to make the managers irrelevant, or quit performing the actions their bosses want.

If you're searching for inspiration on how to build a culture of peer and manager-led recognition, a great place to start is at carrots.com. And the key is to get started as soon as possible. You'll remember the 15 point swing in recognition scores between the Best Companies and those that didn't make a BCG list. It shows that breakthrough teams are built with appreciation, and there's a reason. When recognition is used in concert with the Basic 4, team performance is accelerated, as is personal competence and esprit de corps (the combination that many call engagement). This "perfect storm" carries breakthrough teams more quickly toward their vital goals, which is where we all want to be.

Take for instance the experience of business process outsourcing giant Sutherland Global Services. At this 26,000-employee firm, one of the critical metrics tracked is attrition, because in a people business, attrition is a reflection of employee satisfaction and has a direct impact on the bottom line. "Reducing attrition has always been everyone's job. But showing up to work is not enough. We know that engaged associates are key to providing service that exceeds our clients' expectations," says Iris Goldfein, chief people officer.

So, in 2007, Sutherland put together a new engagement team tasked with only one job—improving employee engagement and reducing attrition. An employee satisfaction survey showed some associates were leaving because they didn't feel appreciated and felt that their managers were not giving them the support they needed. But the survey also uncovered that some employees weren't as engaged as they needed to be to provide what Sutherland calls "platinum-level" service to their clients—exceeding all metrics and providing service that is superior to their competitors.

A Sutherland Global Services executive read *The Carrot Principle* and he quickly surmised that systemic recognition was a key ingredient that could make a big difference in their organization. "Everyone in North and Latin American leadership read and were trained on the ideals found in *The Carrot Principle*," Goldfein said. And they quickly introduced a new recognition program tied directly to their corporate values. "We drove the value of recognition deep into the culture of the organization."

On its face, the ability of an organization to make meaningful change is a great story. But we all know that what matters is focused execution, leading by example, and delivering measurable results. And in Sutherland Global Services' case, they did execute and deliver *results*.

Goldfein says their investments in this recognition program were paid back many times over. "And the organization feels different in the last eighteen months. People are happier. There's a real change in enthusiasm levels. And employee survey results show a dramatic increase: a 9 percent increase in overall employee satisfaction, a 13 percent increase in employee participation, and a big increase in engagement. Those are remarkable movements—statistically very significant."

Dilip Vellodi, chairman and CEO of Sutherland Global Services, regularly visits service delivery locations around the world and attends many quarterly employee dinners that are held in various locations, a regular part of the recognition program. After attending the quarterly employee dinner in Mexico, he said, "It was impressive to see an effective leadership team in Mexico, leading an organization with employees actively engaged at all levels. This is clearly reflected in the superior results that they have been driving on behalf of our clients." It is important to note that their CEO is an active participant in the recognition process.

Not only that, Sutherland's annual employee attrition dropped more than 17 percent in North and Latin America, paying for the recognition program many times over.

Goldfein summarizes: "A well-thought-through recognition program for which you hold your people accountable pays measurable dividends."

Rather than being satisfied with their attrition numbers, Sutherland Global Services looked at it as an opportunity and asked what they could do to improve, knowing that it would have far-reaching implications for their organization, their people, and their clients. Like these leaders, we don't have to wait for others to add the recognition accelerant. We can introduce it ourselves in our teams, our sites, our cities and make the kind of impact that organizations really notice. This is one of those remarkable opportunities, in which doing the right thing for your employees is doing exactly the right thing for your organization.

After all, it's important for everyone who is associated with breakthrough teams to understand that the goal of *The Orange Revolution* is not to unseat good managers. Effective managers play a vital, albeit different role within breakthrough teams. Rather than acting as gatekeepers, leaders understood their function as facilitators, helping to set the team's vision, removing obstacles, securing resources, and encouraging celebrations. We've met managers who provide their employees with a stack of thank-you cards so when they notice something worthy of recognition, they have the tools to do something positive. Other leaders give employees small recognition budgets and invite them to use the funds to cheer on their co-workers.

We encourage leaders reading this book to provide the necessary support, resources, and guided independence for breakthrough teams to succeed. As they do, they will find themselves achieving more than ever before. A leader's greatest success comes by lifting someone else into the spotlight. It's a truth too few managers ever learn.

BUT WHAT IF I'M IN A WORKPLACE THAT STINKS?

On the other end of the spectrum, there are employees reading this book who want to be part of a breakthrough team, but don't think it is achievable within their current organizations. But the truth is, at this very moment, great teams are surviving and even thriving in some of the most hostile corporate environments on earth—we've seen them.

We particularly love the verve of an educational team at a rehabilitation facility for troubled youth. The small group of teachers has introduced an intriguing, integrated approach to teaching. In one of the most challenging, dour workplaces imaginable, three times a week (every other school day) this band of exceptional teachers pursue their educational goals by helping students put on a musical revival. The youth perform show tunes, rewrite scripts to make them contemporary and funny, and then check them for grammar and historical accuracy. The teachers have found a creative way to combine lessons in English, history, and the arts in a way that builds a palpable energy. By the end of the semester, the students and faculty are part of a breakthrough team that rises above the general sense of discouragement pervading the rest of the building.

Every three months they start over with a new set of troubled teens—taking a tough situation and overcoming it. And frankly that is what most of us must do at work. We must overcome, well, work. It's no coincidence that the French word for work, *travail*, is taken from the Latin root "tripalium," an instrument of torture employing three stakes and a lethal dose of fire. Indeed, few of us are bounding out of bed each morning, eager for another day in the cube maze; but we could be, and we're not being Pollyanna when we say that.

Let's go back to the story of the team aboard the *Dechaineux* submarine for a moment. Even under the best of conditions, when your submarine isn't sinking and things are running smoothly, life isn't easy underwater. Confined space, long missions away from home, sleep deprivation, little privacy, they all add up to a stressful workplace environment.

Proving this, a report by the Australian Defense Force Psychology Organization, noted: "All submarine crews report fairly low levels of commitment to the Navy, suggesting many are beginning to lose a sense of esprit de corps with the wider organization."

And yet while these crews have little commitment to the navy as a whole, the majority of these workers report that they do like their work and also like their crew members.

"Respondents reported high levels of teamwork, high confidence in their immediate commanders, and a general feeling of being valued and cared for at the unit (submarine) level. [But] these positive ratings did not translate into higher commitment to the Navy," the report said.

For all of us working in difficult companies or for difficult leaders, there is a significant truth here. Despite the problems inherent in the submarine environment and common in the organization of the navy, the crews feel strong ties to each other and work together well as teams. What does that say about the possibilities for us on land? If our organization doesn't quite have it all together yet, is there hope? If they talk about teams but don't really understand the value of the people on the teams, can anything be done? Yes. The genius of breakthrough teams is that their insular nature helps them withstand harsh environments. They can exist anywhere.

We acknowledge that there is a lot of skepticism about teams today. For those who have yet to experience a great team firsthand, this idealistic talk about breakthroughs can start to sound like a fairy tale. To many, the realities of the workplace aren't unity, engagement, and trust; more familiar are the opposite traits of backstabbing, one-upmanship, and blame. It's unfortunate that the best paths are often camouflaged. Our Basic 4 + Recognition are more than an ideal, however. They are the natural order of things.

The Orange Revolution is an invitation to return to these roots and take charge of our futures. We're not talking mutiny; instead we say the time is ripe for a revolution that starts within you. You can take responsibility for transforming your work and discovering meaning as you nurture your personal competence, adopt the Basic 4, and learn to recognize others' contributions. Along the way, you'll find yourself surrounded by a community of revolutionaries, all armed with their own unique skill sets, and ready to take on the world.

From there, greater meaning in work is just one key decision away: Decide to believe that together your team can achieve anything. That's where we go next.

4

The Rule of 3:
Cultivating a Team

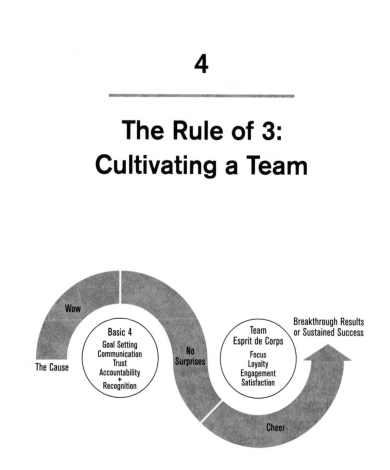

Let's say it's your first day on the job. Your team is meeting "the real you" for the first time. They get the chance to judge you, and the potential impact you'll have on the organization. Quickly they realize you are armed with a solid understanding of the Cause of the organization, and you display your competence and understanding of the "softer" side of business (aka the Basic 4 + Recognition). You let them know you want to transform the world around you; but you can't do it alone.

How can you inspire your team to change the world with

you? Over the next few pages, we'll demonstrate how individuals at all levels can trigger teamwide transformations.

Our story begins with a newly promoted—and very nervous—Scott O'Neil.

It was early 2004, and in his new office fourteen floors overlooking St. Patrick's Cathedral in midtown Manhattan, the National Basketball Association's newest executive was pacing.

From the outside looking in, you'd be hard-pressed to identify the source of O'Neil's worries. After years of hard work, O'Neil's devotion to his personal competency had paid off. His new job as senior vice president of team marketing and business operations gave him direct supervision of dozens of league office employees and oversight of every NBA team's ticket office.

The deal came at a price. It was now up to him and his team to increase attendance in a league where season ticket sales were flat and the new crop of superstars had yet to emerge.

Jump ahead and this story does have a happy ending. For each of four consecutive seasons Scott O'Neil's team was instrumental in NBA franchises combining to set the all-time record for regular and postseason attendance. More than 100 million fans attended games during the period, team sponsorship revenue showed double-digit increases annually, and the team/league dynamic was the envy of the sports world.

But pacing amid the brushed stainless steel paneling and hardwood floors of his office, such success seemed like a far-fetched dream. In the few months since taking over his new job, O'Neil had been traveling throughout the league, meeting teams, assessing the situation. "Things were okay. We had huge brands, accomplished executives, and good relationships. But we hadn't come together as a great team," he said.

Among O'Neil's biggest challenges were the lack of sharing and trust among teams. In this case, the competitive spirit and rivalry between teams didn't end on the court; it carried over into the business side of the league, pitting ticket office against ticket office. When one franchise developed a unique idea to drive season ticket sales, it held on to it as if it were a matter of national security, even though there was no competition for ticket dollars between markets. The local hockey team or twelve-theater movie-plex had a much greater chance of poaching their customers than an NBA franchise three states away.

There were also some communication challenges within O'Neil's immediate head-office marketing team. It seemed that no one wanted to disagree with each other, so there was little dialogue. Instead of taking individual accountability for increasing ticket sales and introducing innovative ideas, team members seemed to be waiting for the new boss, O'Neil, to tell them what to do.

With all of this weighing heavily on his mind, O'Neil slid into his seat to watch the Detroit Pistons face the L.A. Lakers one Friday night that spring. The place was electric. The fans were screaming. There wasn't an empty seat in the house for this marquee matchup. He stared down at two teams pushing and sprinting around on the hardwood—bodies crashing into one another, deft pick and rolls, and more than a few soaring dunks.

As the game neared its final minute, the teams were tied. Suddenly with time running out, Pistons point guard Chauncey Billups shook free of his defender thanks to a solid pick from teammate Richard Hamilton. Billups floated into the lane and sent an arching shot off his fingertips and into the net. The horn sounded. Game over. The Pistons had won. The players all sprinted to congratulate their teammate (aptly nicknamed Mr. Big Shot) on the game-winning points.

O'Neil smiled. It had been a great team victory. And what was so apparent on the court was a level of teamwork that could be translated to his team in New York City.

Success was less about acting as a manager, always forcing and pushing and driving change, and more about playing a leadership role on his team.

After fifteen years in management and with a Harvard MBA, O'Neil knew most business books stressed that a manager should provide guidance and motivation, but all seemed to overlook the biggest piece of the puzzle—when the team is in the arena, on the court, or on the factory floor, the team members are ultimately responsible for winning, not the coach.

O'Neil knew he needed a new game plan for his team. He started with a self-check, knowing that leading a team through an Orange transformation would require the best he had to offer, including personal leadership in goal setting, communication, trust, accountability, and recognition.

The next step, he knew, was to bring the best people he could find into his league office marketing team; and he went looking for the right people. They weren't hard to find.

"When you come into an organization, you find the exceptional people pretty quickly," he said. "They're usually frustrated by the time you get there. I interview as many people as I can and ask them to open up about the things that we could change to make the organization great. The people that I want on my team are saying, 'But I want to . . . ' and 'I think we can . . . '"

With the right people in place, O'Neil called his team together to talk through the opportunities in front of them. Although tentative at first, the team pulled together to outline their expectations for the league's marketing and ticket sales, but also for each other as teammates. Eventually, a small set of team rules began to emerge, not as the new senior vice president dictating change, but as a collective work.

"This wasn't about the boss coming in and saying, 'These are the rules.' That never works," said O'Neil. Instead, it was about building something together. "We debated, discussed, and batted until we got buy-in from everyone."

In the end, the team agreed on three commitments:

Wow. The marketing team would hold itself, and their partners throughout the league, to a world-class standard of performance.

No Surprises. All team members would engage in open communication with one another, establishing clarity of expectations, freely debating issues, disagreeing if they had a good reason to, and sharing ideas.

Cheer. The team would root for each other, which included appreciating great work, providing support, and avoiding disparagement.

Just taking it at face value, it's a good list. And we've found such lists of commitments are created by breakthrough teams around the world. Admittedly the language varies: Instead of "Wow," one manufacturer we work with calls their commitment to high performance "Top Gun." At an East Coast pharmaceutical company "Cheer" is called "Applause."

No matter what their collective commitments are called, the concepts are similar in the breakthrough teams we studied. These basic ground rules hold sway in hundreds of teams around the world. We have culled the best and have come to refer to them as the Rule of 3: wow, no surprises, and cheer.

"There is magic in three," explains O'Neil. "It's three strikes and you're out. Area codes are in three. A three-point shot brings the crowd to their feet. It's three seconds in the lane. Our brain functions in a way that three things are easy to remember and we can draw on them in our daily lives. One value never seems to encompass everything, and more than three is too many to drive and stick."

Most significant, the Rule of 3 is something that can be initiated by team members at any level, within large or small groups. In O'Neil's case, a manager initiated the conversation, but we've also seen it begin organically at much lower levels. In these cases, the conversation starts more like this: "I was wondering if there was a way we could all communicate more about what we're doing. It would help to know what's going on with projects throughout the team, so when we meet with clients, we aren't surprised."

With a little persistence and organization, we've seen these types of benign team member comments prompt real, lasting change within teams. The result is a unit that draws closer to an Orange environment, just like the team marketing unit at the NBA.

WOW

O'Neil's team began their discussion with a question: "How are we going to impress each other?" That predictably led to a debate on regular and postseason attendance numbers and team sponsorship revenue, which prompted a unique commitment. "We decided that when we woke up in the morning and looked at ourselves in the mirror we had a decision to make: 'Am I going to be great today?'" said O'Neil. "When we walked into a meeting we made a decision, 'Am I going to be great in this meeting? Have I prepared properly? Do I have the right attitude? Have I done the research? Am I willing to share and receive?'"

"At the NBA, we said, 'It's okay if you don't want to be great every day, in every way, you just aren't going to work here! There are some jobs where it's okay, just not here.'"

Of course, at the pinnacle of the athletic world are stories of people who commit to be great. A world-class swimmer, for instance, might win the majority of her races by a margin less than a second. Said O'Neil, "It's the extra laps she swims. It's the extra weightlifting she does. It's the same in business: You make a decision to be the best in the world every day, every minute."

If what O'Neil just described sounds familiar, it's because you've probably seen it applied in more than business or sports. For instance, water is hot at 211 degrees, but at 212 degrees, it boils. At the slightly lower temperature you can make soup, but just one extra degree creates steam, a force powerful enough to move a locomotive. In business, it's extra effort in the right direction that powers extraordinary results for breakthrough teams.

For O'Neil and his team, the question, "How can we impress each other?" resulted in a group commitment to put extra effort into being completely prepared each day.

"Our preparation was one way we became really talented and good at what we did. We worked to the bone, and it was absolutely painful sometimes, but we worked and prepared and were equipped for anything that came our way."

That was the price to being world class.

NO SURPRISES

Of course, team member preparation depended on knowing exactly what was going on around them at all times. This type of open communication does not always come about immediately. In the first days within the NBA league office marketing group, O'Neil came to the table ready for feedback, but his team wasn't there. After all, who wants to disagree with the boss? Early meetings were characterized by pleasantries and a distinct lack of debate.

"There was a general play-it-safe atmosphere," said Chris Heck, who O'Neil appointed as a top lieutenant. Heck explained, "We all thought Scott wanted to hear that he was doing a great job. But he took me aside after one of the first staff meetings and asked me to start disagreeing with him. He wanted to open discussions up to conflict, to show that it was a safe environment in which to disagree. It was a great concept and it really worked."

The ability to disagree, without causing offense, is essential to robust communication within breakthrough teams. When dissent is discouraged, the flow of ideas stops. That is damaging enough, but we have also found that a lack of dialogue can interfere with achievement of goals, especially when goals are imposed without team input. In these cases team members feel less responsibility to meet the goals, often feeling that the expectations are not realistic. Conversely, in environments where members are free to help set goals and then speak their minds about the direction, accountability for individual and team goals flourishes.

To foster this openness—and the trust we've found is so vital in the best teams—Heck remembers O'Neil doing a few smart things to spur the team forward: He readily admitted his mistakes, dropped his guard, and was authentic and real. "People are smart and know when you are being yourself and when you are not," O'Neil added.

That decision to lead by example was key. Personally implementing a desired behavior is always the best way to influence others to follow.

CHEER

Of the three commitments, closest to O'Neil's heart is the idea of cheering for each other. But, he warns, cheering is not about pompoms, but generating a confidence that your team members have your back. "It's not about being a nice guy. It's not sitting in a circle singing 'Kumbaya.' It's about proactively looking out for your team members," he said.

O'Neil says he and his team quickly found that actively encouraging each other led not only to better morale, but also more open dialogue and better business results. "If I know you're rooting for me, I have more license to challenge you, to give you direct feedback, and provide suggestions. It eliminates the defensive mechanism that we all have inside."

It also facilitates a culture of individual accountability, because members know their colleagues will hold them responsible in positive ways for their results, and so they are that much more vigilant in fulfilling goals.

Obviously there are some serious business benefits to this type of environment, but O'Neil adds that cheering also creates a place where people love going to work. "Within our team, there was a lot of fun. A lot of very open dialogue. There was a lot of noise," said O'Neil. "We would create ticket sales contests internally. We would have tally boards and try to outsell another part of the team. Every day we'd walk through every single aisle of our cubes and chit-chat with our people, joke around with them. We even had a basketball hoop in the office and we'd encourage people to dribble the ball, to shoot and be a little kid again."

As O'Neil began to feel more confident in the growing esprit de corps among his team, he began to focus his attention more on resolving the disconnect between ticket offices around the league. He knew he had his work cut out for him; but having implemented the Rule of 3 within his league office marketing group, he felt confident in the power of the ideas to overcome the competitive culture and get all thirty offices sharing contracts, ideas, and strategies.

He and his league office marketing team began by demonstrating the principles. "If I learned an idea in another arena or even another sport to sell more tickets, I shared that information. And I expected them to do the same," said O'Neil. The league office's new spirit of openness proved irresistible; and most ticket offices began to share ideas and cheer for the other franchises' success.

Heck said their goal was to have all thirty teams sharing contracts, ideas, and strategies. But, of course, there were some holdouts. "There was a core of about a half a dozen teams that had no interest whatsoever. So we had to create season ticket promotions and sponsorship products that were so good that they would be envious of them, and we didn't allow them access to those products unless they participated. If you didn't give, you didn't get. It was a great challenge; it meant our output had to be world class."

Likewise, they wanted premier esprit de corps throughout the league. To foster a spirit of openness and idea sharing he wanted around the NBA, O'Neil tried a number of unique tactics. For example, while visiting a city, he would invite the local ticket groups to play early morning basketball games on the arena floors. Men and women, young and old, coordinated and otherwise would show up.

"Nothing says togetherness like a 5:30 a.m. wake-up, hopping in a cab, and the sound of a bouncing ball on an amazing stage. More was learned, discussed, hashed out, and laughed about. There were no titles on the court. It is the world's best meritocracy. It really did help build our team."

Said Heck, "There was a vast range of talent, from ex-professionals down to people that could barely dribble the ball. And we had a blast. If you didn't play, people would look at you like 'get over yourself.' If someone said, 'I'm terrible,' we'd say, 'so what?'"

O'Neil claimed during one of our interviews that he would often reverse-dunk the ball during these games. "Well that part's not true," laughed Heck.

What was true, though, was that within only a few months the teams around the league became more engaged, prolific, and goal-focused. They seemed to "play" better together—leveraging one another's strengths, and picking up slack for each other's weaknesses. There was a new energy out there—an aura of winning. And the results for the entire NBA were remarkable.

Says Heck, a tough East Coast native, "I'm not into hokey stuff. It's not my cup of tea. But with Scott it was genuine. You have the New York attitude of, 'I can't worry about somebody else, I've got my own problems.' But it was a complete change of philosophy with Scott's new attitude. You started seeing change in two months and it really came to fruition in six, which is extremely fast turnaround."

"We changed the landscape. They weren't competing against each other anymore, they were helping each other," said Heck. "We went up almost 60 percent in revenue in five years. We put our heads together and got smarter."

Why? Because the team committed to be great (Wow), because they shared everything (No Surprises), and because they learned to encourage each other (Cheer). Three simple rules that created a breakthrough team at the NBA league office, with practices that spread around the rest of the league.

Interestingly, the NBA wasn't the only entity to benefit from the team's success. Word of the league office's team marketing accomplishment spread fast in the sports world, and almost all members have seemed to benefit greatly from the success.

Most of O'Neil's team have since moved on to executive positions. One replaced O'Neil when he left the NBA, Heck is now the NBA's senior vice president of USA Basketball, another is the chief marketing officer for the Pittsburgh Pirates, another is chief executive officer of the Derby County Rams of the English Championship League, another is running a division of Major League Soccer, yet another runs the Los Angeles Sparks of the Women's National Basketball Association, one runs a division of the National Football League, while another is president of the NBA's development league. In other words, the members of breakthrough teams benefit individually when their team does well.

And O'Neil was no exception.

THE GARDEN

In the fall of 2008, Scott O'Neil received an unexpected call. He was offered a position as president of Madison Square

Garden Sports. In this role, he oversees all aspects of business operation for three professional sports teams, the New York Knicks (NBA), Rangers (NHL), and Liberty (WNBA), as well as the Sports Properties area, which includes college basketball, boxing, tennis, and all other sports events held at Madison Square Garden.

And one of the first things O'Neil encouraged his new team at MSG to do—after developing their own Rule of 3—was to introduce a powerful new symbol: in this case, a purple water buffalo.

The odd symbol emerged when a team member found a remarkable video of a buffalo fighting for survival in Kruger National Park South Africa. (You can find a link to the film on our website at carrots.com.) In this very real video captured by a group of tourists, a small family of Cape buffalo walks across the savannah near a water hole, oblivious to a pride of lions they are approaching. When the buffalo eventually spot the lions they are startled and flee. The lions give chase and quickly single out the baby—the slowest and weakest—and bring the smaller buffalo down in a few feet of water on the edge of the lake. To add insult, as the lions try to drag the struggling baby onto dry land, a crocodile emerges from the water and grabs on to the buffalo's leg.

After a few moments the lions are able to recover their prize from the crocodile and drag the buffalo out of the water. Then the shaky amateur video camera pans back to reveal something amazing. More than a hundred buffalo have emerged from the brush to rescue the baby. In the most dramatic wildlife footage you may ever see, the buffalo drive away the lions one by one and the baby is returned to its mother.

O'Neil becomes animated telling the story of this mesmerizing fight for survival. "I think it's analogous to life, certainly to corporate life. We ask ourselves here at MSG all the time, 'Who do you want to be?' You can decide to be the tourist watching it all happen. 'Look, there's a piece of paper on the arena floor,' and walk by it. You can be the lion crouching and waiting for the weak. You can be the crocodile who snaps at someone when they're down. Or you can be the water buffalo. And so when we talk about a water buffalo-type effort, we talk about team play and helping each other and rooting for each other. "And if you come to my office you'll see a big purple water buffalo that stands proudly in my office." And purple? "Well purple is remarkable, royalty. It is different and special and that's who we want to celebrate."

The buffalo symbol, created and embraced by the team, reminds everyone of their shared commitments to wow each other, openly communicate to avoid surprises, and to cheer. It is a unique incarnation of the Rule of 3, and it is extremely effective.

We admit that O'Neil's story is remarkable, but it is certainly not unique. All around the world, individuals are introducing the Rule of 3 to their teams, and spreading the empowerment and esprit de corps of the Orange Revolution among their colleagues. Some are managers. Some are team members. It doesn't matter where a person fits into the org chart, as long as they embrace a set of rules that moves them toward world-class results, openness, and a positive culture.

As Scott O'Neil summarizes, "It isn't fair to say, 'My organization doesn't get it.' We all have more influence than we'll ever know if we exert that influence for good in our teams. Each revolution starts in the mirror."

Over the next few chapters, we'll explain in depth how to embrace the ideas in the Rule of 3. And we'll share some extraordinary examples of people we've met who are using these commitments to influence their teammates and organizations for the better.

5

Wow:
Six Secret Ingredients
to World-Class Results

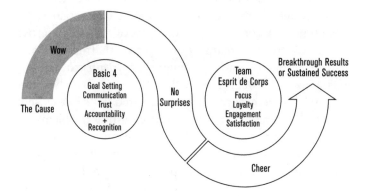

Some teams make it look easy. Why is it that some business departments or groups achieve world-class results and others fall short? Do breakthrough teams comprise individuals with superhero talent, DNA, or drive? Is there a secret to their success?

While we found that breakthrough teams always include competent people, most are not comprised of a preponderance of people with remarkable intelligence or unique expertise. They are not so-called Dream Teams. In fact we met dozens of breakout groups made up of people who, up to that point in their careers, had been more supporting players than stars. We began to realize that world-class results come only partly from *who* makes up these teams, but more importantly *what* these teams *do*. This chapter focuses on what makes these teams break through and achieve real business results.

To back up, we've been researching great workplaces for almost two decades now, and along the way we were curious to cull the similarities between teams that wowed. At first we thought a list of traits might vary significantly by industry—a greater amount of cutting-edge ideas would emerge in breakout high-tech groups, for instance; enhanced compassion in great health care teams; and so on. But what we found were more similarities than differences. Breakthrough teams had some common characteristics.

We found six core traits, and they were consistent across a range of diverse organizations. Teams that are focused on wow results do the following: they *dream* truly ambitious goals; they *believe* in each other and what they can accomplish together; they take calculated *risks* but closely *measure* their results; they *persevere* despite problems or conflicts that arise; and they have a charming habit of *telling stories* that exemplify what they are trying to achieve.

These six core traits might appear at first to be ideological and passive; however, you'll see the teams we've chosen to spotlight apply these concepts with active rigor—helping drive exceptional team performances and inspiring results that are truly out of this world.

TRAIT #1: DREAM

Vinnie Chieco, a freelance copywriter, had been offered a new assignment. He was working with a client who had a reputation for superior results—and this client was about to reveal a new product to the market that would create an impact of massive proportion. Chieco was tasked with giving it a name. When he was sent a prototype, it didn't resemble anything on the market; it was like something from a sci-fi movie. Naming such a radical device would surely be difficult. He needed to communicate both simplicity and revolutionary technology in a single thought. The smooth edges, seemingly button-less device reminded Chieco of a famous line from the movie *2001: A Space Odyssey* where the character Dr. Dave Bowman says, "Open the pod bay door, HAL!" In the film, HAL is the computer that could control the ship. The "pod," in the movie is a spacecraft used for extravehicular activity. Somehow, the word "pod" resonated with Chieco. It seemed to be a perfect fit for Apple's out-of-this-world travel into the future of music.

The release of the iPod has famously revolutionized the music business, and that was exactly what Apple CEO Steve Jobs and the iPod team set out to do; they are an ideal example of a team with a big dream. But it's interesting to note that their dream wasn't entirely original, which in some ways made it even more ambitious. MP3 players had already been on the market from other manufacturers. But Apple dreamed of making a player that would be transformative, that would be world class.

Much like the team assembled by Edison to create a better, long-burning, and safe light bulb, the iPod team was focused on reinvention—building something that would not only outperform all competing products, but would entirely own the market space. And this dream was explicit; during the unveiling, Steve Jobs clearly expressed the team's vision to the media: "It will go down in history as a turning point for the music industry," said Jobs at the time. ". . . landmark stuff."

Let's not get confused at the difference between a goal and a dream. A goal is something measurable, trackable, and is built on analytics. Goals have realistic timelines, are measured by weighing the data, the risks, and the current assets. They are essential to success, but they follow dreams. A dream is bigger—it has no boundaries, rules, or past history. It's focused on transforming business as we know it, and approaching from a direction never pursued—or at least never attained. In dreams, we seek the outstanding change—not just within the products we create but in the results those products inspire. For Apple, the dream was to change and dominate the music industry. And the product (in this case, the iPod) enabled that dream to become a reality—shaking the world with results. It wasn't just the contours of the device. It wasn't just the technology. It wasn't the simplicity of buttons. Apple's dream was so vast that it changed how music was heard, sold, purchased, and consumed. The iPod launched the platform of iTunes. And with such a massive public and music industry shift, the PC world shifted to accommodate as well. This was a dream that defined world-class results.

Obviously, the iPod team succeeded. On January 27, 2010, just nine years after its launch, Apple announced that the 250 millionth iPod had been sold—making it the fastest-selling music player in history.

Given its breakout success, it might seem obvious that the iPod was a great idea, but it really did take dreaming big in order to pull it off.

Consider this: The initiative was launched in 1997, on the heels of a year in which Apple *lost* $816 million. That alone leads to an interesting question for all of us: would your organization, on the heels of its worst year ever, take their best people and put them on a team to design a product so far outside your current business model? Oh, and there's more. Apple at the time didn't have a pipeline of new talent to back up these stars. The company's creative reputation was waning, as were profits, so industry insiders hardly considered working for Apple a desirable career move. Next there were equipment challenges. Apple wanted to

offer consumers ten hours of continuous play before need-
ing to recharge the device, but a spinning hard drive—the
1.8-inch hard-disk drive where the music is stored and was
the iPod's key technology—requires a lot of battery power,
and on top of that it was new in the MP3 space. From an
engineering standpoint alone the iPod was a huge dream.

Obviously the iPod team needed to overcome a number
of hurdles.

Those who signed on to the team were not in the least
bit naïve. Jon Rubinstein, who was chosen to lead the iPod
charge, had a long history in the computer industry—both
in hardware and software. Tony Fadell had started a company called Fuse in the 1990s. One of the devices his company had considered was a small hard-disk-based music
player. His company failed, but Fadell still believed the
opportunity existed to create something with impact in the
MP3 world. Michael Dhuey was an electrical and computer
engineer, recognized as the co-inventor (with Brian Berke-
ley) of the Macintosh II computer in 1987. And then there
was Jonathon Ive, the design guru who had been creating
all of Apple's outrageous appeal.

Rubinstein expresses their commitment to the dream
well as he recalls his reason for coming onboard. Despite
the challenges the company was facing, he remarked in an
interview that Apple could be "the last innovative high-
volume computer maker in the world."

The iPod team is exemplary of all of the traits of breakthrough teams that we've discussed; the skills of each personally competent team member fit together perfectly. They
were all steeped with experience. It was technical savvy
meeting creative brilliance. It was a combination of past
successes meets past failures. It was a group of men who
recognized their individual strengths, but had also gained
a thorough understanding that they could not achieve the
dream unless they realized the strengths of one another.

Dhuey worked closely with Fadell on the hardware

development—particularly focusing on the battery. They needed to create something small enough to fit into the tiny casing, but powerful enough to maintain a charge that would oversatisfy users. Ive, who had been a design driving force at Apple since 1997, was to offer his brilliance to the sleek iPod look and feel, which made such a profound impression that when the device was launched, it instantaneously became an icon of breakthrough product design.

While the process of their breakthrough is interesting, the key point here is that these men weren't afraid to dream—in fact, they were driven and haunted by their vision. Together they changed the way music is delivered; and they did it with the full intention of wowing—otherwise they may have wound up trapped in the world of the marginal, just like their MP3 predecessors.

All the teams we spoke with during the research of this book had specific dreams. That will become apparent as you read on. But they had more.

TRAIT #2: BELIEVE

Sometimes, dreamers get a bad rap. We often use the term to denote a lack of drive, a passive wistfulness. In teams, however, dreaming is vital; it is imagining a game-changing idea. And yet in and of itself, a dream might never be accomplished. The secret is in executing to achieve the big idea.

As we interviewed members and leaders of great teams, we found there was an important step linking a dream to execution: it is *believing* your only outcome will be success. To understand this idea, we talked with one of America's most decorated coaches, Chris Carmichael—the man who trained Lance Armstrong personally for more than fifteen years and led him to seven consecutive Tour de France wins.

Carmichael isn't a coach who tells his cyclists to pedal faster or longer without understanding what they are enduring. He's been there. He was a member of the 1984

U.S. Olympic Cycling Team and was on the first American team to race in the Tour de France in 1986. And he understands the reality of roadblocks—a break to his femur ended his competitive cycling career. But, more than anything, he understands that belief is necessary for success.

"I'm asked often about teamwork and how it relates to winning," says Carmichael. "Building a cycling team is very similar to building any other team, whether it's in another sport or in corporate America."

Inside a cycling team, there are climbing specialists, sprinters, and time trial experts. All of these riders use various strengths and strategies during the race. But regardless of their function, they all need to believe intrinsically in their role in a long race like the Tour: to advance their captain toward the finish line. Typically an entire cycling team is arranged around supporting the captain in his or her quest to cross the finish line first. Team captains are people like Armstrong, riders with the best chances of standing on the podium. And this is where the team's belief is so critically important. If the team doesn't believe their captain can cross the finish line first, the efforts and focus of each member will be marginalized.

Okay, so how does a team achieve such belief, especially with the natural concerns that arise within human organizations. Let's step back a little to understand this question using Armstrong's cycling example.

Before he was an American icon, Lance Armstrong was a strong, up-and-coming athlete who seemed to possess all the qualities of a champion. He was winning races all over the world. He was breaking records. He was at the top of his game. And in the mid-1990s he appeared poised to be a contender to win the Tour de France, cycling's biggest prize. But reality threw in a roadblock for Armstrong—cancer. On October 2, 1996, at age twenty-five, Armstrong was diagnosed with stage three testicular cancer. When doctors found it, it had already spread to his abdomen, lungs, and brain. To save his life, immediate surgery and chemotherapy were required. And at the time, his doctors reported that his chance of survival was less than 40 percent (it was actually much lower).

A year and a half later, after a painful battle, Armstrong's cancer was in complete remission. In January 1998 he had reengaged in serious training, and his sights were set on winning the Tour.

Now step back and think about this for a second. Pretend you're building a team, and you need to convince the team members that their "front man"—the guy or gal you're supposed to support to cross the finish line first—just walked away from death and the most physically and emotionally draining experience of his or her life. Would you believe he or she had the strength to win?

"People like Lance refuse to see limitations," says Carmichael. "Innate talent is important, development of that talent is crucial, but it's the ability and willingness to *believe* you can win that ties it all together."

That's exactly what Armstrong did in this case; he gathered the team and bonded them together with his extraordinary belief. He convinced members to believe in him as their captain. In 1999, a year after getting the all-clear from his doctor, Armstrong won the Tour and continued to win for six more consecutive years—with a team behind him all the way, believing, every time, that they could collectively bring home the prize.

This is a common theme with the breakthrough teams we interviewed. They believe they will win, regardless of obstacles. Barriers drive them to push harder—because common sense tells them that anyone on the road to achieving spectacular results will meet with resistance. It's the belief in the "finish line"—far beyond all the hurdles—that drives them forward to success.

So, platitudes aside, how do you create this level of conviction? How does your team realize that you can win?

And replicate your victories? Can we all read a story about Lance Armstrong and his team—supporting him to seven wins in the world's most grueling bicycle race—and take it back into the office and apply it for ourselves?

Let's look at what made this culture of belief possible. First, understand that Carmichael doesn't just train cyclists. His company, CTS (Carmichael Training Systems), trains teams and athletes from many sports—triathlons, motor sports, hockey, and the list continues. He knows the importance of instilling belief in individuals and in teams from day one. So when a talented cyclist like Armstong was able to face death and then step back into the competition, Carmichael and the rest of the team saw an important first step—a belief from the team leader that he could lead them to the implausible.

Successful teams pick up on that leader's passion and share the desire to win. They understand that they are competing against rivals, obstacles, preconceived boundaries, and their own abilities to believe. It's this level of competition that breakthrough teams revel in—whether it's a sales team striving to see who can put up the most numbers for the day, dueling grocery baggers at your favorite supermarket, customer service reps seeing who can make the most raving recoveries with upset customers, brilliant orchestra players struggling to master a highly technical piece, or a team attempting to overcome their leader's crippling disease. It's believing that together you can overcome hurdles of resources, money, personality, or perceptions. All of these are competitions that exist under the premise and concrete belief that the entire team will win in the end against the real competition—our own doubts.

According to Carmichael, it's this consistent, progressive competitive development that helps create world-class results. "Legacies are created by those little daily consistencies of winning," says Carmichael. "Those little consistencies, together, add up to something enormous."

And that means each time you succeed in reaching a small milestone, you believe in a new possibility. Each time you compete, you begin to believe in the possibility of winning. And each time you win, you believe that another victory can be just as easily won—but now your belief is that you can beat your own best.

Breakthrough teams and team members trust in one outcome, winning—even if their chance of mere survival (as in the case of Armstrong) is less than 40 percent.

It was heartwarming as we conducted this research to listen to team members who shared stories of their belief in each other, like team members at Zappos.com believing they can revolutionize the shoe-buying experience, team members at Whirlpool believing they can transform an engrained distribution system in need of repair, and team members from Apple who not only had a dream, but a core belief that their dream would create unrivaled results.

Belief is taking a confident, if small, step forward to see what's possible, and realizing that all those small steps will result in something much larger. Often belief comes from the vision of leadership, but it can also be ignited by a visionary team member—someone who perceives a better process, initiates a friendly competition, or challenges the extent of possibility by taking a calculated risk.

TRAIT #3: RISK

As any gambler knows, in order to win, you have to be willing to place the big bet. As the saying goes, "You have to be in it to win it." In business terms, of course, big bets can be risky, especially without adequate forecasting, planning, or upper-level support for your idea. And yet when multi-million-dollar business wagers do pay off, legends are made. We travel to Somers, New York, for an amazing example.

When Rajendra Gursahaney introduces himself he extends a hand and says, "Hello, I'm Guru." His real title is Pepsi Beverages Company's senior director of engineering, the honorific "guru" has been thrust upon him by his peers—partly because his first name was unpronounceable to them and Guru was a convenient condensation of his last name, and partly because everyone at Pepsi Beverage North America considers him the world expert on bottling. By this point he has accepted it.

Now Guru is truly brilliant. And he is not built to be self-effacing about that fact. "I consider myself a damn fine engineer," he said. Such directness in his lilting Indian accent is quite charming. But even with such confidence, Guru knows he can't build world-changing bottling systems alone, especially when this self-proclaimed "cowboy" likes to take risks to improve the process. To wander into uncharted territory requires his and many other minds working together.

Case in point: the reason we're meeting with Guru. Two years ago he took an extreme risk when he formed a team that would either revolutionize the bottling industry or cost his company millions of dollars.

To understand this story, we need a short lesson in packaging science. Putting a microbiologically sensitive beverage like fresh tea into a plastic bottle has some inherent risks. Noncarbonated drinks are vulnerable to bacteria if they are not properly bottled, thus most companies use what is called "hot fill" technology. The beverage is manufactured and then heated to a temperature that destroys any microorganisms. The heated drink is then poured into the bottle, and that destroys any bacteria residing on the bottle's inner wall.

This technology does have its drawbacks. When a hot beverage is added to a bottle, plastic tends to deform. And when the drink cools with a cap on (which it must to keep out contaminants) the bottle can contract. So bottlers must either use a thick plastic that won't deform (which is expensive, heavy, and creates more environmental impact) or they must add vacuum panels that contract as the liquid does (which is expensive and creates a bottle that is no longer perfectly round—think Gatorade or Powerade).

In 2006 the problem was exacerbating as plastic prices increased.

Guru said, "I wondered, can I put something in the bottle, like a harmless gas, that expands as the bottle contracts and mitigates the deformation? That way, there would be no more need to make a thick-walled bottle."

Hmm? He had the dream. Now, would science back his belief?

At a beverage show in Chicago that December, Guru was walking the aisles looking for a technology that might answer his question. He passed a booth offering nitrogen dosers, a machine that adds a dose of nitrogen to bottles. Many food and beverage products contain nitrogen, an inert, harmless gas. Beverages like Aquafina contain a raindrop of nitrogen that removes oxygen and gives the bottle its nice firm feel. But since a nitrogen raindrop is almost minus 400 degrees Fahrenheit, everyone knew it couldn't be added to a hot drink, as it would instantly vaporize and fluid would bubble out. Drinks like Aquafina are filled at room temperature or lower and the bottles undergo an ozone sterilization process before the nitrogen is injected.

Guru decided to put a team together that could design a way of putting nitrogen into a hot bottle, with thin walls, at incredibly high speeds—up to 50,000 bottles an hour. He knew the company was about to roll out a new product line in Russia with Lipton Tea. As always, the company was concerned about the cost, weight, and environmental impact of thick plastic bottles. Guru wanted to take a risk with this new product line.

"I went to my boss, John Thibodeau [vice president of Worldwide Engineering], with the idea of a hot-filled nitrogen bottle. Nobody had ever tried it in our industry. It was a massive risk. John asked, 'What happens if it doesn't work?'" Guru admitted that not only would Pepsi lose time, they would have spent considerable money buying a bottle-blowing machine they couldn't easily redeploy.

We've often noted how upper management at progressive organizations such as Pepsi encourages a degree of risk taking, as long as it based on the type of well-founded analysis that Guru had undertaken. "But this was a significant decision," said Guru. "To fail would mean reversing and buying three hot-fill-rated traditional machines at a cost of $7 to $8 million, not to mention months of delay."

Thibodeau remembers the risk assessment that followed. "I asked Guru a lot of hard questions about the technology, how it would be different from current cold-fill systems, what was the point of no return, what impact would this have on the launch if the idea failed?"

Guru gathered additional research and set check-in dates to align with the expectations of the organization. And he did the economics. If the idea worked, it would not only save millions per year per line in plastic costs, but could actually help the planet in a remarkable way. He added, "I know it's a risk, but I think our team can make this work."

Thibodeau informed the organization of what they were about to try. And he told Guru that he would "fully support the team through the process."

That weekend Guru attempted to enlist his first team member, an associate from one of the world's largest bottle-blowing manufacturers. The man said no. "He told me he had no faith that this would work. He said if this was so simple, someone would have definitely done it by now. It shook me up. He said you are going to fail big-time, don't even try it."

Monday morning Guru was back in John's office. "I said, 'These guys are experts. They've been manufacturing bottle-blowing machines longer than I've been alive.' I wanted to be honest about the feedback they were giving me. John looked at me and said again, 'What do you think?'

I told him I think we can do it. So he said, 'Go ahead, I'm with you.' It was amazing to have support like that."

With his own belief and that of his boss, Guru assembled a team of people who weren't afraid to risk, knowing that Pepsi would back them either way. He gathered the team members at a test site in Hamburg, Germany. They came from Pepsi, Lipton, the bottle maker, the nitrogen company, the fileing machine company, and from Russian Operations team (the end customer that would be most impacted by a delay in rollout if the technology failed).

This team of six worked for almost fourteen months in the laboratory. On a bench they improvised an assembly line. After one man filled a bottle with hot water, it moved to the next station, where a small dose of nitrogen was added. Next another person attached the cap. Finally, the bottle was dunked in a tub filled with ice. The team then studied the shape of the bottle, twisting it in the light, pulling out calipers, measuring every square inch.

"We experimented with weight, the type of resin, the thickness of bottle, material distribution, different shapes, processes, all with a brand manager sitting by to make sure the bottle looked good and felt good to the touch after the ice bath," said Guru. "It was slow work when you are working one bottle at a time, one person filling, one guy putting in nitrogen, one guy putting the cap on, and one guy dunking."

Finally, after fourteen months, the team had a bottle that withstood all the technical and aesthetic requirements. Not only were the marketing people from Pepsi and Lipton happy, so were the engineers. There was a significant reduction in weight from a traditional hot-filled bottle.

But would it work on a real production line? This time using hot apple juice, the team ran five thousand bottles in a rented facility just to see what would happen.

Guru remembers, "We sat around that night as a team, talking. We admitted the test was not perfect—all the bottles were not the same. Some were hard and perfect, but a lot were soft. We looked at the data, and then I looked each person in the eye and asked, 'Can we maintain process parameters? Every bottle must be exactly the same. If we cannot be consistent every time, we fail.' Every person replied, 'We can do it.'"

The next day an order was placed for the first filling line. By the time "our machine," as the team was calling it, arrived in Russia, the challenge was consistency.

"For the first four weeks, the line was a catastrophe. We had enormous wastage. Ten percent of the bottles were soft and not fit to put into the market."

Knowing their reputations and now millions of dollars of the company's money were on the line, the team worked late into the night for six weeks to determine the problem—tinkering with fill levels and nitrogen doses in an attempt to get the system working properly. Finally, a team member suggested running the line at a lower speed with a high-speed camera monitoring the operation to see if a small amount of nitrogen was missing the bottles. "We couldn't see it with the naked eye. But that helped us get the nitrogen to dose precisely each time with no spillage."

Bingo. The last problem was fixed, and the number of rejected bottles dropped from 10 percent to one-tenth of a percent, which is normal in the industry.

"So it was a success story," Guru concluded with a laugh.

To get an idea of the impact of this breakthrough team, here are some of the numbers: A traditional 1.5 liter bottle weighs 63 grams. Guru's team made a bottle that weighs 48 grams. That's a cost savings of about 2.2 cents per bottle. And remember, these lines produce up to 50,000 bottles an hour. Three lines have already been installed in Russia, so Pepsi Bottling forecasts savings of $2.5 million per line per year in plastic costs alone, adding up to $7.5 million in annual savings. And the environmental benefit for all of us is substantial.

Remarkably, Pepsi Beverages Company has decided not to patent this idea, but instead is letting the entire industry benefit by sharing this technology with anyone who would like to save money and the planet.

"We consider it a win-win," said John Thibodeau. "Not only has it saved us cost, it's the right thing to do from an environmental perspective. We reduce the amount of plastic we are putting into the bottle, which reduces the carbon footprint of having to produce the resin for the bottle from a landfill and recycling perspective. It's a great example of a team of employees willing to take a risk and the company allowing them to do it."

In 2009, Guru was awarded PepsiCo's "Best of the Best" Sustainability Prize, recognizing his efforts to reduce energy consumption and landfill impact. In Guru's typically direct fashion, he admitted that he didn't deserve the prize alone, so he shared the reward with the people on his team.

"This just goes to show you, if you get a group of people together who are like-minded, who know they can take a risk and you have their back, you can pretty much make anything happen." Guru laughs again and is off.

While risk is not the most popular word in boardrooms, improvement and creation demand it. It's interesting that in the conversations we had with breakthrough team members for this book, a similar insight emerged time and again: Individuals who created Wow for their current organizations admitted to being stifled in their past. Many reported having great ideas that, when they brought those ideas to leadership, were rejected—often because of the word "risk." Breakout teams see risk differently. They know risk is necessary, and they understand the impact—both positive and negative—of taking one.

TRAIT #4: MEASURE

An Olympic athlete is on the treadmill, seeming to float effortlessly at a speed that would catapult most of us to the back of the room. Attached to the runner's body are monitors—some measuring heart rate, and some measuring oxygen intake and lung capacity. A coach, holding a clipboard, steps up to the athlete, reaches forward to the treadmill's control panel, and slowly turns a knob that increases the belt speed even further. The runner unbelievably accelerates. And, with timed consistency, the coach continues the process. Each time, the runner—an elite athlete—meets the challenge with ease. And then, a plateau is reached. The coach finally pushes a cool-down button and records the final data while the athlete catches her breath.

In this new world of sports training, everything is monitored—lung capacity, recuperative powers, heart rate, hydration, enzyme levels, and the list continues. And, because of all that monitoring, coaches can know exactly when and why the athlete will hit a plateau and reach fatigue. This process then extends to the race—does the runner suffer from anxiety, is she motivated by spectators, and is she influenced by weather conditions, travel, and so on.

The point is; on a serious sports team all stats, achievements, failures, and challenges are recorded—there's a scoreboard, because a team or an individual can't improve unless you know "the score."

Two years ago, U.S. Foodservice, Inc.'s sales people knew the game—they just didn't know their "score." They were sales athletes, but many did not know if they were world class.

As background, this company dates back to the mid-1800s. U.S. Foodservice provides everything edible, from apple pie to zucchini, as well as things to eat and cook with, from spatulas to paper plates. On any given day you might see a U.S. Foodservice truck pull up at a neighborhood grille, five star hotel, or your local school district.

Of the company's 25,000 employees, approximately 5,000 are tasked with what they call "street sales," selling to independent restaurants, hospitals, hotels, schools, and the like. Because this is a mature market for the entire industry, street sales at U.S. Foodservice had been flat for a few years, and with the economy in a tailspin the horizon looked bleak. Luxury item purchases such as trips to restaurants were dramatically down in 2008 and '09—with some experts reporting the industry would expect losses of 12 to 15 percent, and many restaurant owners expecting losses of 40 percent. With fewer people going out to eat, there was simply less food to deliver.

Most in the food service industry hunkered down and focused on tried-and-true methods to stay in business— they made more cold calls, lowered prices, and so on. None of that worked. But a team at U.S. Foodservice tried something different: implementing a set of detailed performance measurements that helped generate hundreds of millions of dollars in new sales during the worst economy in decades.

"We were looking for a strategy that would increase our street sales by 50 percent over time," said Mark Eggerding, senior vice president of street sales. And to a veteran sales leader, he knew that meant understanding their customers better than ever. That would mean sales people would need to get smarter, more targeted. Sales leaders would need to have a better grasp on what their people were doing day to day. And a new scoreboard would be needed to help keep score. In other words, every sales person would be hooked up to the Olympic sensors.

Eggerding had ideas to implement this type of change, but his corporate group had tried rolling out massive new programs before. "They never gained traction," he admitted. In some cases, the tools were not what the field wanted. In others, the tools were solid but the field just wouldn't adopt them. "Typically the field says, 'Here comes another flavor of the month from corporate, so nod and smile, and eventually something new will replace it,'" he joked.

So instead Eggerding's leadership group chose twenty-two people from the sales field to form a team. The group was tasked with not only fulfilling management's vision of developing a new way to sell using a customer relationship management (CRM) system, but would also identify the best ways to use the system to drive sales and then train all five thousand field people on how to use it. The team was called Foundations, because what they would introduce would be foundational for everything going forward on the street side of U.S. Foodservice's business.

Team leader Steve Horan met with his group. "We decided we wouldn't sit in a laboratory at corporate: the ideas would be generated in the field. We knew the role of the Foundations Team would be to identify the best sales ideas that actually work and have positive metrics with them, and then take those ideas to the rest of the organization."

That's a relevant point. Management wanted to implement this new CRM system, but they wanted this team of sales people to help them shape how to use this technology to accomplish the goal. That's breakout thinking for most organizations, which are used to letting field people focus on selling, while corporate people put new initiatives into place.

Eggerding says, "Philosophically the team members got it right away. That this wasn't about a new spreadsheet or big brother watching with a lead management system, it was about helping our customers succeed and transforming our own organization."

Horan said the group started by thinking of their challenges when they were in the field and how could they be overcome. The team realized they would better know how the sales team was doing and where improvements were needed if they could use the CRM system to track these four core areas of the business: net account growth, customer penetration, account profitability, and sales management.

While these may seem about as interesting as drying paint to you and me, they are as important to the well-being of a corporation as your vital signs are in a doctor's visit. As a business, you won't be alive very long if you can't add more accounts than you lose, if you don't find a way to sell more to your current customers and make them profitable, or if you can't manage the daily activities of your sales force.

The Foundation Team was locked together for months as they developed the program and training. Eggerding smiles when he admits that this team of sales people are "all very competitive types." We assume that's code for "people who normally might compete to get their way, attention, or power rather than working together." Nevertheless, that was the challenge—to take a group of highly competitive individuals and get them to cheer for each other and the organization as a whole rather than competing with each other, which—let's face it—is core to most sales people's nature.

"We used some techniques to build the team approach and rally them around the cause," he added. "For instance, we trained them as one unit. We weekly recognized their success, even when the team members were out training in the various divisions. We even kept up the camaraderie by setting up an internal blog where people could post about the good things that were happening and the challenges."

Ahh, instead of leadership keeping score, it was the team chalking up winning points!

As for the deliverable, the Foundations Team developed a series of online uses for their new technology, allowing sales people to share leads and track current clients with their managers. "So field people and district managers are really working as a team to create new business opportunities," said Horan. "It was really happening."

But it didn't stop there. They also implemented a customer business review process to regularly sit in front of more customers than ever before. Ironically, this not only facilitated stronger relationships, but it gave someone else the opportunity to keep score—the customer. And when customer impressions are measured, it can lead to important insights.

Foundations also leveraged a tool within the CRM to help identify customers who were slowing their ordering or showing other signs of discontent. "Our industry churns a lot of customers. We open a lot of accounts and we lose a lot. Many customers want to stay loyal but need help, and often we don't see the white flag. So Foundations implemented an SOS process: Save Our Sales. It's a way to connect with customers, identify their problems, and keep them happy," said Eggerding.

The new system allows sales people to help the client with an 'aspirin a day,' so to speak, rather than, as in the past, sales people pulling out the paddles only after they lost an account to see if anything could be done to save the day.

With the new tools in place, the team began rolling out the Foundations process corporate-wide in fall 2008. Team members spent three weeks in each division. But the next challenge was convincing sales management in the field who believed their division's process didn't need adjustment. "If a division really wasn't on track, we first showed them the math behind this," said Horan. "We'd see that they weren't engaged in, for example, our ideas to slow customer churn. We'd show them the math that their churn was two times higher than the divisions that had embraced the process. We'd then ask, 'What opportunities do you think there are to get engaged, and where do you think we have a miss that we can work on?' It was a push-pull conversation. The division preferred that kind of honesty. But we couldn't have it if we didn't have the data behind us."

"They knew you can't just hand off a program, you need to deploy it in an organization and you need to work through it with people," said Eggerding. "We can't be seen as a SWAT team that drops in and leaves. Even today we do a check and balance. If we see a number drop, we check back in with the division president."

The field came to see the value of the new measurement tools, and ultimately embraced the methods. "We had a process that didn't just sound good, it actually worked," said Horan. "My team has carried the bag of sales people and sales managers. They began to engage with the division from the president on down and worked with them to build the process that we knew would work."

Of course, a scoreboard comes with accountability and transparency, and that can be unnerving to many. Every sales person and manager in the company is now rated against core metrics, so they can see where they stand in their district and the country. The Foundations Team was well aware that this was likely to cause tension, but we've found in our work that such openness is essential in building a culture of accountability and responsibility. Tension is actually necessary at first to bring about change—but soon after it is adopted teams thrive on it.

"One of the things that has made change possible is the alignment and transparency throughout the organization," said Horan. "We now all look at the same report: our CEO, the division president, and a sales person."

And the results?

"They are amazing," said Eggerding. "We had been even or behind in net account growth until we introduced this process. Last month alone we were up 10 percent in net accounts." We asked Eggerding to think about the last time U.S. Foodservice was up 10 percent in a month. He shook his head. "I don't remember that ever happening."

Eggerding added that the company also measures market share, "We've ticked up significantly last year. That's had a big impact."

"Umm, yeah," we replied. "So street sales really increased last year, during a recession?"

Eggerding nodded—a nod. "Yep, we saw significant growth.

"We also now measure customer touches. So we know how many customer business reviews are done, how many

SOS [Save Our Sales] white flags are raised, and how many leads we have across the country. And we see they are moving in the right direction every month."

Eggerding is still nodding at this point in the interview. He has good reason to.

As for the rest of the Foundations Team, many of the original members have been promoted. They are, after all, the heroes in this story. Interjects Horan, "People are now drawn to the team. Today there are more people who want to be on the team than we can possibly support."

As interviewers, we were amazed to watch both Eggerding and Horan. They had a dream. They helped create belief within the team. They took a risk. And they created a scoreboard for the team. Yet, even though they did everything perfectly, they still seemed amazed at just how massive the results were.

"Foundations has been industry changing," said Eggerding. "We've changed the thinking of our sales people. They now look at the business differently. Today, people are working more closely together for the common cause of the customer. This team has delivered a credible product into our organization and the industry that's never been done before."

Stuart Schuette, chief operating officer, summed it up this way. "Let's put to rest the fallacy that success is due to luck or chance. My colleagues have set the standard for excellence in our industry. In today's market, everyone is looking for a differentiator. Having a world-class way of working with one's customers is what sets the U.S. Foodservice Sales Foundations Team apart from the rest. They have done an exceptional job of establishing and maintaining customer relationships, securing new business, and working as a team with others who share our vision for 'going beyond the plate.' For this, they have earned my gratitude and a place in the U.S. Foodservice 'hall of fame.'"

TRAIT #5: PERSEVERE

Every team hits roadblocks. Some push the team off course, others reduce the team's output, while some challenges actually force the team to disband. And yet great teams find a way through the inevitable hardships. How do they do it? The best answer is this: persistence. Breakthrough teams continue running toward the goal, even when mistakes are made. If their team member falls, they pick him up. If they drop an assignment, they pick it up. They don't dwell on mistakes.

Whatever your business, there are crisis situations that your team faces—where a member misstep could derail a goal. And yet most corporate teams have tendencies to place blame as opposed to helping their teammates pick themselves up and refocus. For those teams that learn how to keep going, some of the best cases of Wow occur during the recovery process.

While this is primarily a business book, it would be naïve to think we could only learn from business teams. In fact, to illustrate the persistence of great teams—and the removal of instant finger pointing—consider some of the most brilliant recoveries that we have been able to see every Saturday night since October 11, 1975. Broadcast live out of Studio 8H in New York's Rockefeller Center, *Saturday Night Live* is one of the longest-running television programs ever—and it's big business. The show is composed of live comedic sketches—typically lampooning current events and famous figures—and features a cast of comedians and a guest host. Just one forgotten or misspoken line during a skit, even a giggle, can derail the entire production, revealing what a gutsy, high-wire act the show really is. But what makes the "live" mistakes so enticing to the viewer is not a stumbling comedian but the brilliance of recovery.

In one now famous episode from the late 1970s, film actor Charles Grodin was guest host. With lines that were clearly being ad-libbed from cast members and their host, Grodin was encouraged during the show to play a daft bungler who doesn't think the show is live and consequently treats every sketch like a take in a film that can be repeated until he gets it right—no matter how often the players reminded him that there are no do-overs on live television.

In a now classic sketch near the end of the show, John Belushi has finally had "enough" of Grodin's bungling and delivers a solemn speech about the importance of professionalism and the craft of acting—made all the more hilarious by the fact that Belushi is wearing a bee costume and his silly antennae bounce up and down when he talks.

Of course, this level of understanding, recovery, and persistence is easy to spot in a high-pressure live situation like SNL. However, again, these qualities seem to elude many of the teams working in corporate America, perhaps because the spotlight doesn't always demand instant recovery. Nevertheless, all mistakes demand team perseverance. This aspect of Wow was extremely clear with most of the teams we interviewed for this book—great teams don't dwell on the mistakes, they forgive and continue moving forward.

Consider this next story from the music industry. It's an example that shows how great teams persevere to reach world-class results.

Their sound was hefty, thumping, and emotionally charged—raw, with grit resembling heavy metal, but with the perspective that appealed to mass audiences. They created an arena-ready rock sound that wowed fans worldwide, producing three multiplatinum albums between 1997 and 2001 that sold more than 25 million copies.

The rock band Creed was a force in American popular music. Front man Scott Stapp's brawny baritone voice seemingly monopolized airtime on radio stations. Songs like, "With Arms Wide Open," "Higher," and "My Sacrifice" climbed charts with impressive ease. The band was on top of the world.

It appeared as if the members of Creed had encountered near perfect synchronicity—rhythm, melody, and harmony. It seemed as if they drove one another to the next level of success as they pushed creative boundaries, developed fresh concepts, and musical inspiration. Truly they achieved world-class results.

But there was something missing. And when it was exposed, Creed crashed.

Put four musical masters in a room who share a passion for greatness and see what happens. It should be magical. Watch them rise to become arguably the most popular band of the decade and you'd think the magic—and esprit de corps—would continue to swell. Well, it didn't.

By 2002 internal squabbles surfaced. In 2004 Creed officially broke up. Some reports claimed the lead singer Stapp battled addiction and personal demons. Other reports said the feuding existed due to other tensions—creative control and song credits. And others said it was just personality differences.

As drummer Scott Phillips told the press, "There wasn't ever a point where anyone was like, 'Alright, I'm done with it.' It was more a question of what exactly is happening?"

The entire band was confused—the issues were clearly present. The solutions weren't. However, any way you view Creed's issues, the truth of the matter is the same: the band wasn't persisting. They were placing blame, and letting their teammates fall further from the goal.

Stapp went on to record a solo album. The other members—drummer Phillips, guitarist Mark Tremonti, and bassist Brian Marshall—stuck together to form the group Alter Bridge. The former Creed members experienced some success, but it was marginal compared with their status together.

A few years passed. And fans from around the globe finally began to believe the finite words of Tremonti when he said publicly, ". . . Creed will never, ever happen again."

Sadly, those sentiments are heard all too often when great teams split. Emotions run high. Words are exchanged. And the bright lights that once exposed the brilliance and potential fade, often leaving team members eternally searching for new team members to rediscover the magic.

Creed, however, has a different story to tell—an epiphany that should have, and could have happened long before all the turmoil set in. After almost six years of separation, the former members of Creed did something we find common in breakthrough teams—they dropped their hostility, began to communicate openly about their differences, picked up their teammates, and persisted.

"We realized what we had built was more important than any of our individual quirks," Tremonti told the media.

The band went back into the studio with fresh material. They hit the road to tour for the first time in six years. And fans everywhere waited for the unveiling of the band's next great journey—a new album, aptly titled *Full Circle*, and the album's first single suitably called "Overcome."

"In order for us to write and create as truthfully and honestly as we did in the past, we needed that bond, that trust, to exist between us again," adds Stapp. "The sincerity of these songs reflects the rebuilding of the friendship," not to mention the rebuilding of a powerful business team.

The takeaway from this story is that even breakthrough teams are going to experience conflict and failure; but when all's said and done—after the viciousness, the dropped balls, and missteps—great teams understand the value of persistence, don't focus on mistakes, and regroup to again create optimum results.

Obviously, the emotions and big personalities of a rock band may overshadow the daily battles in an office setting. But remove the guitars and bright lights and we see it time and again in corporate America. Consider Steve Jobs's departure from Apple and his return—to his team. Consider Martha Stewart's brief hiatus and return. Although she made a mistake, her team helped her rise again. Breakthrough teams are persistent.

TRAIT #6: TELL STORIES

Of the six traits of breakthrough teams, the last was the most surprising. As you'll see, great teams create a narrative. We witnessed it over and over in the most successful businesses we visited. As teams innovate, they tell their stories again and again. They are partly their history (which sometimes becomes mythology), but they also explain to others who they are and why they do what they do.

Take this example told to us by Arte Nathan, senior human resources officer of the Wynn Resort.

Team chemistry is something Nathan—and owner Steve Wynn for that matter—takes very seriously. One legendary story in the organization is an experience Wynn and his family had when on vacation in Paris. They were staying at a Four Seasons, and breakfast had been delivered to the room. His daughter had ordered a croissant, but she only ate half of it, leaving the other half to nibble on later that day. Wynn and his family left the room to explore Paris. And, upon returning to the hotel, his daughter began thinking about that croissant. But when they entered the room, the pastry was gone, taken by housekeeping. She was disappointed. Housekeeping assumed the half croissant was trash. Or did they?

A light was blinking on the room's telephone. It was a message from the front desk of the Four Seasons to the Wynn family. The front desk clerk stated that housekeeping had informed them that they had removed the half croissant from the room, assuming that upon return the rightful owner of the croissant would prefer a fresh pastry. So the front desk contacted the kitchen to set aside a croissant, and room service was informed that upon request, they would need to deliver the pastry post haste.

"What makes this story so powerful?" asks Nathan. "The level of teamwork and communication between different departments is simply amazing. All participants understood the end game—customer satisfaction. And everyone accepted their role in making the experience fantastic. These are the stories that Steve Wynn shares with his teams—and you can witness that level of teamwork at any of his properties today."

For us, the Paris croissant is a powerful example of cultural storytelling. Any employee who hears it immediately knows what the organization means when it says "customer satisfaction." The takeaway is not literal. No one thinks, "Okay, when there's a half-eaten croissant, be sure to leave a message with the front desk." Obviously, it's a deeper understanding than that. It clearly means that employees are empowered to be creative, intuitive, thorough, and generous.

We also suspect that for Nathan, telling the story is a way to weed out prospective workers who simply don't get it. Anyone who hears the croissant story and thinks that level of service is over the top is probably looking for work in the wrong place.

At Zappos.com, too, the stories are flying.

In the buttoned-down corporate world, this unique company is making a difference by being, well, different. Just ask them. Sit down with a Zappos employee long enough, and you'll hear them giggle about the customer service rep who answers the phone with, "Good morning and thanks for calling Zappos.com, where Elvis was once said to be in our warehouse looking for a pair of blue suede shoes." They may also regale you with an anecdote about the rep who welcomes customers with, "It's a zippity doo dah day here at Zappos."

At Zappos.com, the remarkable level of its customer service—which has so much to do with the company's phenomenal success—is fueled by telling of stories of the kind of superior, and wacky, service the company wants its employees to provide. It's a fascinating last trait we found shared by breakthrough teams—reciting both stories of their own successes and using the stories of other breakout teams to communicate their commitment to world-class results.

At Zappos, the tales are shared in break rooms, meetings, customer visits, and especially in new employee training. All new hires spend their first month learning how to answer customer calls and pick orders in the warehouse, regardless of their position. Each class might have a new software engineer, the chief legal counsel, or someone in facilities, warehouse, or housekeeping.

Maura Sullivan, customer loyalty manager, told us, "The most effective way for us to explain to these new people about our mission 'To Live and Deliver Wow' is with stories." In fact, every new-hire training is rich with recounted tales of exceptional compassion, creativity, or humor.

Sullivan had more than a few such stories ready when we met with her. She started each by setting the scene: "It's not a big deal to have a customer return a pair of shoes. We do it all day long. But one caller wanted to return a pair she'd ordered for her husband. The rep asked if anything was wrong with the shoes. The customer explained that since ordering them her husband had been killed in a car accident. It affected the rep. When she got off the phone she told her lead that she'd like to send flowers and a card to this customer, saying we have her in our thoughts. The supervisor said it would be no problem. The customer was so touched that she blogged about the gesture, and that blog was forwarded to thousands."

Sullivan adds another such tale. "We respond to every email we get here except auto replies, 'Sorry, I'm out of the office.' We typically delete those. But a month ago a woman on our email team took the time to read the out-of-office messages. In one, a customer wrote that she was out of the office for a three-day breast cancer walk. The rep wrote the woman a card saying, 'I really appreciate what you are doing by supporting this good cause. I wish there were more people like you.'"

Again the customer had a large online network of followers. She immediately posted her amazement that a shoe company would acknowledge her sacrifice, even though her own family hadn't.

"These stories help new hires realize how empowered they are to make decisions on their own," said Sullivan.

And Sullivan was hardly the only one at the company who kept us entertained with such specific examples. Christa Foley, the recruiting manager, told us this: "Every place I've ever been has the nightmare payroll manager that everybody's afraid to talk to when they've made a timecard mistake. But our payroll manager tries to do everything in the world she can to help you. If you walk into our payroll office you have a fantastic time. She still gets payroll out every two weeks, so that we pay people correctly, but everything happens with a very different attitude because of that Wow value. As a company, we insist that our payroll manager, just like everyone else, delivers Wow service."

When was the last time you heard or read about how fantastic a company's payroll manager treated her co-workers?

All of this storytelling is in an attempt to help employees follow their cause to give Wow service. Foley says, "Deliver Wow through service is our most important core value, it's what our company is all about. The stories we share help people understand they can give it in different ways. Somebody might make a customer laugh whereas someone else may hear a dog barking in the background and talk with the customer about that."

In fact half of each performance review will be based

on the employee's ability to live the values like Wow (the other half is on technical performance). So new hires listen closely to these wonderful anecdotes; and they take the culture seriously.

As a result, says CEO Tony Hsieh, Zappos people are able "to do something that's above and beyond what's expected, something that has an emotional impact on the receiver. We seek to Wow our co-workers, our customers, our vendors, our partners, and in the long run our investors," he said.

Hsieh put co-workers on the front of that list for a reason. He believes focus to service starts inside an organization. He believes the Wow stories begin internally, and once passed through the halls, inspire others to create and tell Wow stories of their own.

Many on Wall Street might suggest that storytelling is marshmallow soft—a sweet, fluffy concept that doesn't truly add to the bottom line. However, Zappos' remarkable financial success speaks to its worth.

Customer loyalty manager Rob Siefker says, "The Zappos difference is about more than just numbers. Stories encourage us to find little ways to improve interactions. Let's say we answer 80 percent of our calls under twenty seconds. That's a metric that's great. The question then becomes, how can we infuse those interactions with more fun or creativity? Or, how can we do a little bit more for our customers within those moments to increase the level of engagement?"

So Siefker and his fellow leaders position the tales they tell to encourage originality, even a few yucks. Either way, stories are shared—internally and externally.

Sullivan told us one more story that speaks volumes about the strong ethic of their unique brand of weird, funny customer service: "A man called in and asked our rep to refer to himself in the third person, and he referred to himself in the same way. The customer said, 'Jimmy needs a new watch. Could you help Jimmy get a new watch?' Our rep went along with it. He said, 'Jonathan would be happy to help find Jimmy a new watch.' The caller then said, 'Jimmy's got a big fat wrist.' That was classic. It was so funny."

But there's more to the story. The caller, aka Jimmy, was a clandestine reporter who wanted to see if Zappos really was as fun as it claimed to be. Needless to say, "Jimmy was convinced. Jimmy wrote an article. And Jimmy used the transcript of the call in his article."

"At another company the rep probably would not have gone along with it, thinking this guy's crazy, but our guy just had fun and we got a lot of positive press because of it," said Sullivan.

We speak and train at companies all over the world, and we're always amazed at the great stories we hear that sadly aren't being made public—the hospital food service team that went from worst in the nation in customer satisfaction to best, in just six months; the aerospace team that is winning multimillion-dollar defense contracts by asking five-star generals to play with toy tanks; even the tender story of the millionaire business owner who sat every day at a different work bench and asked about his teammates' families.

Breakthrough teams tell such stories frequently and with passion. It is a secret ingredient of their success. The power of the stories is in their specificity and vividness, which are the very elements that make them so memorable. They get repeated—typically with the same enthusiasm in which they are told. Stories are vital in helping individuals understand how world-class results are achieved and in making the possibility of doing so believable. Such tales have a way of perpetuating success. The listener retells the story and, more important, internalizes its message and becomes part of the story.

Stories transcend Wow results and lead us into an environment of open, intriguing conversation.

6

No Surprises: Mastering Orange Communication

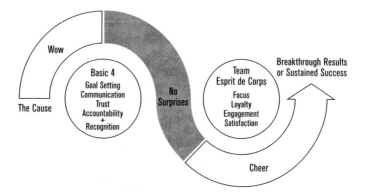

Imagine buckling yourself into a $30 million high-performance jet, launching into the sky at 500 miles per hour, and performing complex flight maneuvers just inches away from five similar aircraft operated by world-class pilots. Such amazing exhibitions require a stellar team, the Blue Angels, the epitome of teamwork. Since its first flight demonstration in 1946, the team has performed shows for more than 455 million spectators, 13 million last year alone.

After World War II, the team performed in order to keep the public interested in naval aviation. By the end of the 1940s, they were flying their first jet aircraft. As technology changed and jets got faster, the Blue Angels continually upgraded to newer, sleeker, and quicker aircraft. Over the years, as the United States has participated in various armed conflicts around the world, the Blue Angels have been deployed. Today, however, the team's mission is to enhance the Navy and Marine Corps in their recruiting efforts and to serve as an ambassador for those branches of the service.

We interviewed Scott Beare, a pilot who flew with the Blue Angels for three years—the maximum time permitted—to learn about the secrets of the team's success. "When you join the Navy, they don't send you to Teamwork 101," says Beare. "Of course, boot camp in any of the armed services provides a fantastic foundation—everyone wearing the same clothes, sleeping in a bunk room, organizing your military-issue belongings exactly the same as the guy next to you. Boot camp brings people to a realization that they have become one team instead of many individuals. Yet when we're talking about breakthrough teams—that synergy that you feel when you understand and build on the people around you—even the military doesn't prepare you for that. I was part of many teams, but none like the Blue Angels. There I experienced a synergy that is indescribable."

The Blue Angels are exemplary of much more than the skills necessary to fly; they exhibit qualities that are enviable and would benefit any organization that is trying to reach new heights. Think of the levels of trust, cooperation, and individual competency that are paramount to their safety in flight. And is there a team anywhere that risks so much with such a small margin of error? Nevertheless, the reason we sought out one of their stars was this: small communication mistakes in an air show can lead to huge errors, and the manner in which the Blue Angels have institutionalized open, honest, and constant communication makes them especially suited to illustrating the importance of No Surprises in fostering great teamwork.

Of all the teams we studied, they were the most striking example of open and honest communication. There are literally no surprises on the Blue Angels team. Each member knows exactly the roles and responsibilities of every other team member during every single mission, and if any problems or confusion arise during a flight they are dealt with quickly and efficiently before members strap on their flight suits again.

Scott Beare revealed that one of the keys to their phenomenal success is that they have a well established process of communicating. The team engages in a constant review of their efforts: planning before an event, monitoring during, and analyzing after each event.

Winging it, so to speak, is out of the question.

HOW ANGELS COMMUNICATE: PRE-, PRESENT, AND POST-

Performing precision moves high above the earth requires complete clarity about the plan for each flight and each team member's responsibilities. The logistical planning for each event is intense and reviewed with the whole team intensively. "We hold a brief before each event," says Beare. "Even though we've flown the patterns a million times, we sit down and discuss every maneuver, and how we'll execute. We discuss the demonstration in absolute detail."

The communication is continued during the shows, as pilots keep up a steady stream of focused chatter with each other and the ground crew every minute of the performance. The dialogue focuses around something they call *The Center Point*. "No matter where we're flying, a geographic point is chosen at the location, a point of reference used by all pilots to execute maneuvers. It's the center—the place we all understand, and it's never compromised. Obviously we need to know exactly where each member of the team is, every second of that performance."

Such preparation and focus on the common goal before and during the event might be expected, but Beare explained that their intensive communication continues even when the jets are back on the ground. "After the demonstration is when the real communication begins. The crowds have left. We've shaken hands with all the spectators who wanted to meet us. We've taken pictures, signed autographs, and represented the legacy of the Blues. That's when we go into debrief—because every performance can improve."

The Blue Angels discuss every maneuver performed that day. They go over every mistake, every miscommunication, every slight variation, and every detail, and they do so in an environment of total honesty.

"If I was flying too low or a half-second off my mark, either I tell the group, or they tell me," says Beare. "We discuss everything in the debrief. It's not a short meeting and it's definitely not an afterthought. Communicating those details drives our synergy, our trust in one another, and ultimately our ability to perform."

No matter how talented the individuals on a team may be—and you'd be hard-pressed to find a more gifted group than the Blue Angels pilots—if they are not communicating with one another openly and honestly they can get off course. For the Blue Angels, that would spell disaster. And though the consequences for most teams are less starkly dangerous, all teams will run into trouble at some point without this kind of introspection.

We've all seen violations of the No Surprises rule in our workplaces or in high-profile media stories, where communication is withheld, lost in translation, or just misunderstood. What happened when John Lennon finally admitted working on a solo album while still with the Beatles? What happened to President Richard Nixon and Watergate? And, just recently, consider the story of the CEO who was accused of withholding information and paying out billions in bonuses to employees before his company's acquisition. The results of his "surprise" were devastating—to his company's reputation, the team members who suffered from his actions, and their customers. Of course he broke the cardinal rule that says: Never Surprise the Boss (or his soon-to-be new bosses). But, even more important he broke a rule that was more devastating: Never Surprise Your Team.

We all are human. We all make mistakes. We miscommunicate or undercommunicate, and sometimes we eliminate—either purposely or mistakenly—communication altogether. That's why forecasting mistakes that could happen, planning to overcome those mistakes, honestly admitting when mistakes do happen, and taking accountability and ownership to ensure they don't happen again are critical.

Beare recalled an incident during his career as a fighter pilot that makes this point dramatically: an example of when the lack of communication could have led to an unintended war.

He was on a confidential mission in the Middle East. Beare's orders were to fly behind an unmanned electronic warcraft plane (EP3) and protect it at all costs. Somewhere in the middle of the Persian Gulf that morning on an aircraft carrier, destiny had its own orders.

"In the Navy, we always fly with a wingman," says Beare. "But that day my wingman's plane was down, and only he had been given the details of the mission—it was a last-minute thing. So I was going out alone—with just an order to support and protect."

Beare at the time was an F-18 pilot for the U.S. Navy. He had flown countless missions before this day. He knew his job well and the responsibilities that accompany that level of commitment. But, this day, Beare was in for the surprise of his life.

"The EP3 was headed west," said Beare. "We were off the coast of Iran and all of a sudden it started heading east—right into a no-fly zone. I couldn't have any communication because it might give away our location. So I did what I was supposed to do—I followed the EP3. And I kept my mouth shut."

Beare says that he wasn't over the no-fly zone for long when he noticed two Iranian F-14s approaching. Within seconds the planes were within forty miles—a distance too close for comfort when traveling close to the speed of sound.

Luckily, the EP3 turned back out over the Persian Gulf. Confrontation avoided. "Obviously we made it out safely," says Beare. "But it was a tense few moments."

Of course, Beare says that situations like these are extremely rare in the Navy. "Everything is so well planned that when these situations do arise, it's good to know our men and women are trained to know how to react. But these situations shouldn't happen. And anytime there's a problem with communication, it needs to be addressed, so it never happens again—in the Navy, in the workplace, and even in our personal lives."

We see team communication failures all too often: One team member has a hidden agenda. Another is pointing fingers and placing blame. One is sugarcoating a negative situation. One simply says nothing at all. One worries about the consequences of speaking his mind. Another has a transformational idea but has been ridiculed in the past. What should be honest communication leads a team to a failure to correct problems or the withholding of vital information that could benefit the entire team.

As we interviewed teams, we found some common consequences of failing to live the No Surprises rule.

First, there were missed deadlines and opportunities. We spoke to members of a design agency. Shannon, a designer, told us that the team learned of a pitch to win a significant new contract at the last minute, a result of a breakdown in communication between the business development members of the team and the creative folks. They had time for just one meeting before the pitch, where a member of senior leadership joined the meeting late and encouraged the team to "pull together to create something astounding," then left. With no time for brainstorming meetings, and a full plate of existing clients, the team decided they only had time to show a collection of work from previous clients. They didn't get the job.

Another consequence of a culture of surprises is a palpable increase in anxiety and mistrust. A team member at one large non-profit described toxic mistrust amongst her team-members. The agency's dysfunctional director kept assignments vague—often assigning numerous staff members to work on the same projects independent of each other. She would also pit members of the team against one another. The result was a team that not only didn't trust the other members, but didn't trust the manager either. "Every day the anxiety is immense," She said. "It's impossible to know if your colleagues are out to stab you in the back or if our boss trusts any of us."

Surprises also marginalize engagement. In one-on-one conversations, we were told by numerous employees at a large transportation company how big-picture communications were rare. They were putting packages on trucks, but they had no idea how that impacted the world, how their team was performing in comparison with goals or peer teams, or how the company was doing overall. "We're not supposed to talk to one another during work," said one employee. "I've been here for eleven years, and I just tell all the newcomers to shut your mouth and make it look like you're busy."

Finally, surprises can cause customer dissatisfaction—with lost or confused orders, an inability to live up to promises, a lack of answers, and so on. We had an interesting example, in a reporter who had worked at a television station in one of the country's top five markets. The woman had interviewed neighbors at a crime scene, and one of the witnesses had said some obscene words on camera. The reporter logged the tapes, using time frames that included the swearwords, but assumed her photographer would edit the offending words out. No such luck. The obscenities were aired that night. The public was offended, the station's reputation was damaged, fines were levied, and both the reporter and photographer were let go. As this reporter and the station learned, the cost of surprising your customer (or audience) can be economically detrimental beyond measurement.

The point, as with all these examples, is this: in business, surprises and communication failures cost us money. But honest and continuous dialogue allow teams to carry out their missions according to plan. The trouble is that in most teams openness is taken for granted, simply because we expect execution will go as planned. But the reality is rarely that simple. It takes some effort to create an environment that allows teams and individuals to realize their potential—members acting on behalf of the team, and for the good of the team.

"Open communication fosters trust," says leadership expert John C. Maxwell. "Having hidden agendas, communicating to people via a third party, and sugarcoating bad news hurt team relationships. Your goal should be to speak truthfully but kindly to teammates."

Throughout our research for this book, we spoke with numerous teams and senior leaders who were searching to find the answers that can pry open the secrets to clear and honest communication. And although processes did vary from team to team and organization to organization, we dug up a few simple truths that were shared by all.

ACKNOWLEDGMENT AND RESPECT

On the teams we studied, a culture of No Surprises was ignited when team members became aware of, and learned to respect, each member's responsibilities and personal goals. In great teams members understood the difficulties each person had to deal with—professionally and even personally. No player, role, duty, or difficulty seemed too small, too unimportant, or even too important. Not surprisingly that respect extended well beyond the workplace. We heard team members telling us how they admired their teammates inside and outside of work. They shared bits of information as, "Bryce is trying to run a marathon," or "Did you know Sue was made president of her kid's baseball league?"

So how do breakthrough teams build cultures of acknowledgement and respect? First, they learn multiple roles. On many of the teams we followed, including the Blue Angels, it's common practice for team members to be trained in many facets of the team so they have an understanding of the entire organization. On the Navy's elite air team, for example, even the team physician and ground crew rate and critique each performance. At some of the firms we visited, all new hires spend weeks learning various roles in customer service before they can start their jobs in finance, IS, or human resources. When everyone on the team understands responsibilities and potential difficulties the other players face, they are more aware of the impact of each person on the whole.

During one of our focus groups, a software developer in his early thirties told us about his team that was redefining his company's back-end systems: "There is a certain intensity with our team that's not for everyone. People want to be a part of it, but some come and are spun out as fast they join. They have to understand there is no my job and yours. One day you may be working on the budget, and tomorrow it may be handed to someone else because she has time and you are needed somewhere else."

Numerous companies we interviewed created shared experiences outside the office to facilitate such a cooperative, respectful culture amongst team members. Shared experiences build rapport between employees and often shed light into each person's true personality. Experiences mentioned were everything from offsite team lunches to in-depth retreats. One group walked every year as a team in the Susan G. Komen breast cancer walk, another attended intensive leadership development camps together.

Kevin Smith is a State Farm agent and business owner in Chicago. He believes acknowledgment and respect have long reaching business implications: "Everything we do, from each sale to the way we treat others, will define our personal brands. And everything we do is about the team, the entire team. That includes their families, friends, and passions. For instance, I've found it more important to remember my teammates' spouses and kids' birthdays. When you involve the entire team, you make a deep impact that inspires people to do things that even they couldn't believe they were capable of."

Those aren't just pretty words from Smith. This type of respect has helped lift his team to numerous state records for new insurance applications in a month, and in 2009 his business was up almost 30 percent despite the recession.

AVAILABILITY

Being available for each other is critical to ensuring all team members share information about potential issues and have the opportunity to ask tough questions. When managers and team members aren't accessible, team members feel like islands unto themselves. This leaves room for hidden information, lost productivity, incorrect outcomes, and disengaged team members.

Similar to a parent who has no time for his children or significant other, a lack of accessibility sends a set of negative messages to the people at work that we need the most: that they aren't important to us or the team, that their peers are more important than they are, and that their ideas, questions and concerns aren't relevant. One spirited team member we spoke with told us about his former job at a nutritional supplement company where his boss's door was always closed. This guy was so fed up with the lack of accessibility that he wrote up his resignation, sent an urgent email requesting a meeting with this manager, and then still had to wait three full days to quit—because she was "too busy."

So, how can you build a team culture of accessibility? First, open your doors. Zappos.com is a terrific example. CEO Tony Hsieh and all of senior leadership sit in cubes without doors on "Monkey Row," a line of cubes with a jungle canopy overhead. It's hard to believe, but despite the fact that the company has 1,700 employees and annual revenue in excess of a billion dollars, there are no offices, no doors. But there is a lot of communication.

Liz Gregersen is administrative assistant for this group of executive primates. In typical Zappos weirdness her title is the Time Ninja. She says, "Normally you'd have to go through an assistant to get to the CEO or COO. But people just walk up to them or email. It doesn't matter who you are."

Whether it's online, face to face, telephone, or even a suggestion box, Orange Teams have forums—meeting places where all team members join together to share status updates, struggles, expectations, and kudos. A trucking company out of Philadelphia told us that they use an online message board where team members can post and read updates of fellow drivers. A team member at Yum Brands told us about their stand-up meetings before every shift where any question is fair game. And a creative team at an educational consulting firm in Arizona told us how they gathered every Tuesday night at a local eatery. "The conversation isn't always focused on projects," said Gary, the managing director. "Sometimes the team just gathers to say, 'We're in this together' and ask each other what's going on outside of work." Obviously being available can take any shape or form that works best for your team. The forums are simply a time or place where all team members can congregate and communicate.

ACCEPTING IDEAS

All great ideas were, at one time, considered off the wall. Within breakthrough teams the free flow of communication is facilitated by an openness about sharing ideas, and an ethic of encouraging even the strangest concepts to see the light of day. On these teams we found a general appreciation of the fact that new ideas—even bad ones—can lead the team to greater success, and that challenging the status quo periodically is important.

The trouble is, most of today's common workplaces aren't accepting of the flow of ideas. Hierarchies exist that stifle most ideas from the ranks. And some have even told us in the past that they had ideas that could save money, accelerate productivity, or eliminate challenges, but felt they "weren't in the position" to risk their jobs. One fellow called it the "foxhole" syndrome: keep your head down in your foxhole or it will be taken off.

How can you build a team culture that encourages creativity and improvement? The first step is to actively seek ideas. Consider Sue Promane, director of supply chain at Whirlpool Corporation in Canada. She told us that when she was hired some employees weren't sharing within her group because they thought that the feedback wouldn't be welcomed. It's a common concern, but Promane knew her team would not accelerate without the team members' full imagination, so she began not only asking for ideas, but rewarding them—even if the ideas weren't applicable.

It's a great concept: every idea can and should be appreciated. After all, team members are sharing with the intent of helping the team or the organization as a whole. A VP from a manufacturing plant told us that he solicits ideas from all the employees via a "good old-fashioned" suggestion box, but then rewards each generator with a small expression of appreciation. He says, "We read every suggestion at our weekly meetings. Yes, we get some fantastic ideas on our policies or products, but we also get some ideas that are pretty funny. Either way, good idea or bad, I hand write letters thanking each person for contributing. That's really what it's all about—the effort. And we were surprised once by an employee who had a history of sharing some of the craziest ideas ever. One of his ideas was absolutely brilliant. It's saved us a lot of money."

This vice president found that innovation comes from creating a culture of candor. We shared the stage recently with Jonathan Blum, senior vice president of public affairs for the restaurant giant Yum! Brands. During his talk he explained that one of his company's core values is "we seek truth over harmony." That's great advice that should be shared with every team. The Orange Teams we observed had come to expect an open and continuous stream of ideas—good and bad. And, frankly, we've seen—in our own professional lives and through the teams we've studied—that bad ideas received in a candid culture can lead to the best ideas. They open dialogue and help people focus on what a good idea might be. Many of the teams we spoke with insisted that ideas that challenged the status quo were just as worthy—if not more valuable—as those ideas that supported the typical way of doing business.

Consider again the supply chain group we spoke with at Whirlpool Corporation in Canada, identified by the CEO as a "game-changing" team in his organization. Many of the employees admitted that they had suggestions that would have improved processes, but because the ideas challenged the status quo were afraid to share them. That is, until Promane came in and encouraged and rewarded an open flow.

RESPONSIVENESS

It's a haunting fear during adolescence that we'll reveal to that special someone that we like them and have them respond negatively, answer with an ambiguous "hmm," or even worse not respond at all. Because the fear of "no response" is so intimidating, people often withhold their thoughts and feelings. Responsiveness is a critical component of creating a team culture of No Surprises. And today this idea is even more critical as so many of the ways in which we communicate are technology-based. Through the volume of emails, texts, instant messages, phone calls, and Web meetings a lot of communication gets lost or avoided (because it can be). The face-to-face pressure of sharing on tough issues is often lost—it's so much easier to push "send."

It's vital to understand how corrosive it can be to put off responses until later. Within breakthrough teams we found unwritten rules of prompt response. Great team members do not leave their teammates hanging in limbo. They respond immediately, and they actively hold one another accountable to communicate. If a team member isn't responding he is confronted. If members aren't responding with enough attention, the team acknowledges (with candor) the miscommunication and how it could affect the team's goals. Lack of responsiveness—whether it be the timing or quality of the response—can be interpreted by members as a lack of respect, a lack of interest, laziness, or a signal of frustration. And these factors can lead to mistrust, misalignment, and team anxiety.

To build a team culture of such responsiveness, Kim Jacobson, art director at Red, Inc. in Idaho, told us that her team has a rule of never allowing team questions to be left unaddressed. "I'll get back to you by the end of the week is a fair response," says Jacobson. What's not fair is silence.

Since email, cell phone ring tones, and all the latest technologies are equipped to prioritize communication, great teams program alerts and folders to ensure team member communication is prioritized. E.G. Carlstrom, a sales rep for Southern Wine and Spirits in Southern California, told us, "Although those of us in the field are working separately, it's critical for us to respond to one another. I may have a question from a client about a product that another rep could answer immediately or vice versa. So I always need to know when one of my team members is calling." In this case, responsiveness and prioritizing drive sales.

BROADCASTING VITALS

On the Orange teams we studied, vital signs are broadcast for the world to see. Deadlines, goals, responsibilities, and progress are always in view, and members are aware of the objectives of their fellow members and the team as a whole. In fact, this was a consistent practice across all the breakthrough teams we interviewed. Each had implemented some sort of broadcast medium to communicate vital measurements and goals.

This is obviously not the norm in most teams. One employee we spoke with summed up the problem in her group succinctly by saying, "Nobody knows what's going on in our team—at all." Enough said.

So how do you create a team culture that broadcasts vitals? In short, speak to the masses. Metrics affect everyone, and they should be crafted and communicated in a language that everyone can understand. Deadlines, although they do not always affect every single person, are valuable timelines that provide insight and accountability to all employees as to why, how, and where other people on the team might be currently focusing. If all members know and understand that one of their teammates is under pressure, they can help alleviate other duties, responsibilities, and stresses.

Some companies take this up a level, ensuring openness

of metrics at not only the team level, but corporate-wide. "One thing that's helped us stay together is our openness with our numbers," said Loren Becker, a supervisor of training at Zappos. "We have finance classes where we teach every employee to read a balance sheet. Last year, a lot of people in the company wondered how we did a billion dollars in revenue but didn't turn a big profit. Where did the money go? So we showed everyone that about half of our money went to buying the goods we sold, a quarter went to rent and salaries, a quarter went to advertising and other expenses. Pretty soon there's not a lot left over of that billion." That communication about the company's financials has fostered teamwork in cutting costs. Says Becker, "I hear our people saying, 'Maybe we shouldn't put these papers in binders, maybe we can do without these pens.' They try to trim expenses down. We've become a lot more cost conscious because of our openness."

Within the Carrot Culture Group we broadcast vitals via numerous media. We send out a detailed revenue spreadsheet to everyone once a month, and our logistics team sends out a weekly update with current projects, responsibilities, and achievements. We all listen to Chester's weekly podcast, we also hold "all-hands" stand-up meetings twice a week, and we have plenty of other meetings to keep everyone feeling they are connected to our deadlines and goals.

OFFER HELP, ASK FOR HELP

It's a cutthroat world, right? Asking for help in business or at the office is viewed as a sign of weakness—that you're not a master at your craft. But that's not the perception we found on breakthrough teams. The programmer we heard in a focus group said this: "I reach out to other developers, I ask for their opinions, then I show them how I've incorporated their ideas. I ask, 'Is this right?' We create a bond that way."

As we observed within these great teams, offering help to team members—even if a colleague is unsure the help is wanted—opens dialogue; it often leads to team members opening up about problems they're running into, and over time it leads to enhanced trust. It's not about *appearing* as if you're committed to the team, it's a real sign that you *are* committed to your team and the success of your teammates. Rolling up your sleeves and helping a teammate also helps team members understand more about one another's roles and responsibilities and specific challenges.

And on the flip side, asking for help allows others to understand your struggles, hurdles, fears, and concerns so that they can participate in doing whatever will help to solve those problems. Contrary to the "old-school" thought that asking for help shows weakness, it actually reveals strength and shows respect to your colleagues. It shows you trust their advice and insight, and opens the door for them to, in return, ask for your insight and advice.

While great teams hold each person accountable for his or her deliverables, they likewise hold them accountable to get the help they need if they can't solve a problem or achieve a goal on their own. Managers and other team members often initiate this helping conversation simply by telling their teammates where they could use help. This is often done during team meetings where all are present and can witness the open dialogue. Yes, it would be easier to email one person directly and ask for help, but it doesn't reveal the possibility to others.

Back to Becker at Zappos, who explains how leaders in his firm will intentionally give new employees a task they can't possibly do themselves, with the hope that they will have to ask other people for assistance. "We don't tell them up front they'll need help, they have to figure it out on their own." But that tactic has paid dividends. In Becker's department, he has eleven trainers working on courses. "In the beginning, we wanted to hold tight to our projects. But we validate our folks when they bring ideas from another team member. Now when we are developing a training we realize we need someone who's good at PowerPoint, someone who's analytical and good with a spreadsheet, and the three of us will come together to develop a class. Now our people can't wait to share their ideas." They can't wait to help, and be helped.

CREATE FACE-TO-FACE TIME

It may seem old-school, but looking at the whites of their eyes works wonders—it's one of the most valuable traits of No Surprises cultures. The breakthrough teams we studied gather regularly in person, face-to-face, to discuss current responsibilities, struggles, successes, and even fears. Managers make a point of circulating to talk with their teams. Team members go out of their way to talk with other members who may not be currently working on a shared project. They eat together. They take breaks, play ping pong, or foosball, or chat together. And it is clear—seeing the groups together—that communication extends far beyond words.

Open communication is more than messages sent and received. There is a value—a bonding process—that happens in greetings, sharing ideas, and working with someone that cannot be achieved via any other method. We all somehow understand that value when it comes to children, family, or friends, and yet in business it seems alien.

But over and over we found that great teams *want* to spend face time with one another. While we admit it is hard and often expensive, teams with a large number of remote employees still must create opportunities to bring everyone together for intensive sessions that bond and provide clarity. Togetherness—it's one of the most powerful messages we can send.

7

Cheer: Up

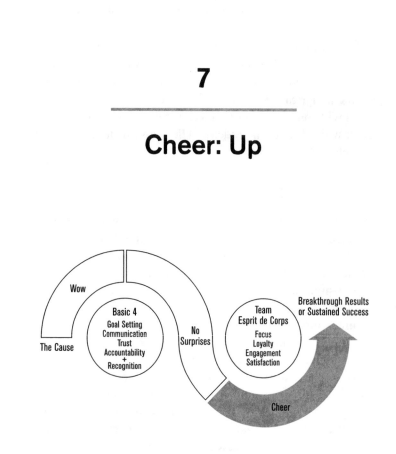

We've been inside organizations that had perfect theoretical teams and departments: leadership communicated effectively, strategies were clear; workers were talented, everyone knew the goals, shared commitment, and was motivated to high performance. Everything was neat and tidy. And then . . . little fights broke out, disparity of opinion wreaked havoc, gossip ensued, meetings became increasingly less efficient and effective, and resolve sagged. Finally, the team broke down—kaput.

As you can probably attest, calling a group of people a team is no guarantee that they'll come together and act like a team.

Team dysfunctions happen because we are people, and that means we sometimes act in regrettable, unprofessional ways. Sad, but true. And these individual problems become team problems as the people fail to coalesce into a single-purposed body. As any manager can tell you, a part of every day is spent working on teamwork issues such as: Mike is backbiting about Debra's work ethic. Shy Aaron is getting a bad rap as being aloof from the group. Matt, a top performer, has become a prima donna that no one wants to work with. Ruth is in a bad mood a couple of times a week and takes her irritation out on the two new team members. We could go on and on.

There are so many potential problems lurking within teams, we can understand a manager wanting to throw in the towel on the entire idea of cooperating. Many have done that, to their own detriment. Instead, we take you on a clear-eyed review of why teams struggle interpersonally, a pointed attack toward the specific issues that undermine teams, and finally, an initiation to a unifying act that will bring the team together.

Let's start with the harmful side. A breakdown in a team is usually the result of one or more of a half dozen common problems: infighting and ego; seemingly irreconcilable differences of opinion; misdirected ideas of competitiveness; cultures of blame; inappropriate hierarchies of power inside the team; and unaligned values of the individuals that are not in sync with the organization's goals. It's human nature for any given group to occasionally squabble. After all, looking at the litany of team troubles above, it is easy to find similar issues on an elementary school playground, in a college dorm, or a corporate boardroom. We can be too eager to fight over misunderstandings, too stubborn when we could be conciliatory, too focused on our version of being right, too competitive, too quick to point fingers, too willing to climb over others to get ahead, too focused on "me" instead of "we." These personality-based team troubles are the result of individuals who lose focus on what the group is trying to accomplish. They aren't bad people. They've simply forgotten why they are working with others in the first place.

Now what of the manager? We certainly cannot ignore the part played by a leader who exploits personal weaknesses. When individuals are disagreeable, does the manager condone demeaning behavior if the person is a good performer? Is risk so frightening in the culture that the blame game is the first reaction to any perceived failure by a teammate? Are there hierarchies of power so pervasive as to make nimble teamwork impossible? If these problems are allowed to flourish, they become like weeds in a garden, choking out productive growth. Take blame, as just one example. If a manager allows a team member to throw a co-worker under the bus successfully, the message to the rest of the team is clear: survive at all costs. Teamwork is derailed until a new leader intervenes to discourage dissent, or excessive competition, or aggressive maneuvering—helping teammates work together, competing against *outside* forces, not internal.

If a team is to be sustainable, more positive leadership is required.

The facile answer, then, is to make everyone the same, a team of equals. The marriage-of-equals team is a fairy tale. The dirty secret of teams (that we've saved until chapter 7) is that they are messy and unbalanced. On some other planet perhaps all team players share the same power, expertise, ambition, and motivation, but that's a rarity here. A much better way to think about teams is using the image of the inner workings of a mechanical watch. There are wheels, springs, gear teeth, pinions, levers, and shafts, which all need to perform specific tasks and be in balance with each other. Are the parts all the same size or shape? No, but they have the same ultimate purpose.

Thus, there are big wheels and small wheels on every

team. They have different talents. They are paid differently. They are at different stages of their lives and want different things out of the group. We shouldn't try to pretend otherwise. But that shouldn't lead to imbalance. We shouldn't accept that infighting and resentments based on these differences are an inevitable feature of teams. After all, the more time we spend trying to resolve squabbles between team members, the less time there is for doing the work of the organization.

Teams that are relatively free of tensions do exist. In our study, we found that breakthrough teams were at their heart supportive. They were relatively free of ego and comprised members who seemed genuinely interested in helping each other achieve.

If we were to be asked for one unifying action that we saw in these teams that would help other teams—as disparate as they are—come together, we would sum it up in one word: cheer.

Cheering is the secret sauce that can create a spirit of camaraderie so strong that the act of supporting each other becomes second nature, where the vast majority of pettiness and finger pointing stops. Unhealthy competition abates, blame is diminished, and values start to fall into line when people back each other as peers. Of course, Ruth might still be moody from time to time, and Aaron may still be shy. But, for the most part, the behind-the-scenes maneuvering and scheming ends; the conflicts fade and the old baggage that hobbles the team dissipates when people cheer.

To be truly effective, cheering has to be cultural. The company has to nurture it, reward it, make it part of every day. It has to be as natural as breathing.

In the most productive team environments, employees are seen, supported, and praised as human beings, not merely workers. And it is appreciation (or recognition) that is the key cheering factor that unlocks commitment, loyalty, drive,

and ultimately, success. As their talents and efforts are rewarded frequently and specifically, they become more respected by co-workers. Those colleagues also strive for the same treatment. It isn't a competitive reflex; they merely want a bit of cheer too.

The more embedded cheering is in the organization's daily life (through personal and group celebrations of success), the more teamwork flourishes naturally. Sounds easy enough, right? Then why is it so rare? Why do so few groups root for each other? Perhaps because we don't realize how important it really is to our collective success. If we all did, we'd all be reaching for our pom-poms.

Back to managers for a moment: The leaders of the great teams we studied have come to rely on frequent cheering of individual and team success. Often this started with a CEO who had an epiphany regarding recognition and its influence on teamwork. The consequence, if the recognition has been done in the right way, is greater unity among teams—as they now have the tools to appreciate each other. The team members also begin acting independently, finding creative ways to think. All of which is an effort to appreciate anyone who accomplishes tasks tied to team and corporate goals.

It's important to note that we are not talking about traditional forms of pay-based rewards. The year-end bonus and the dangling possibility of a once-a-year raise are not motivators, but satisfiers. And when used alone, without award programs, they give employees the impression that monetary praise is everything. Thus, most employees are open to any offer, however small, that can top the current employer. What we are talking about is personalized recognition with tangible awards that reinforces an individual's important role on the team. There are caveats, however: recognition needs to be frequent, specific to your core values, and timely in order to be effective. But is it ever effective!

And yet recognition as a top-down activity is only a part of the solution. People working on a team need support, not only from the top, but from every direction. This is where many teams falter. Without a culture of cheering for each other, peer-to-peer, teams cannot possibly achieve a true atmosphere of cooperation. It's a question of reach. A manager can only do so much, see so much, thank so much. Weigh that philosophy against a culture that doles out cheer frequently with peer participation, and you'll find cheering is the power that keeps the team working together.

Our research uncovered stories of teams that have seen the power of recognition as a driver of cheer. The stories show how appreciation for great work can galvanize everyone toward a common goal. Seems like a snap, doesn't it? And it is at Zappos.

SNAPS AT ZAPPOS

Online retailer Zappos has been as high as number 23 on *Fortune* magazine's "100 Best Companies to Work For" list, so they know a little something about cheering for each other. We talked through this concept with atypical call center managers Rob Siefker and Maura Sullivan. Siefker told us about SNAPS recognition that happens in their Customer Loyalty Teams. By the way, SNAPS stands for Super Nifty and Positive Stuff. "We do SNAPS in our Zuddles (or Zappos huddles), and we just had one earlier," he said.

"We like to put Zs in front of things," Sullivan quipped.

Siefker explained, "The lead supervisors and managers hold Zuddles with our teams at 9:15 and 3:15 on Tuesdays and Thursdays. It's quick, what's going on in the call center, are there any big ticket items we need to discuss, big news that we need to pass down, and then at the end we do SNAPS. There's a little box in the call center and people write things that someone else did that was really cool.

These are read during the Zuddles and then the person is publicly recognized on the spot. It's peer-to-peer. Then we all snap our fingers. (Sullivan and Siefker both demonstrate for us, as if we've never seen snapping, and they are laughing as if they just thought up the idea. They are so darn upbeat we can't help laughing with them.)

Adds Sullivan, "It's been a fun way to make sure we're recognizing each other, even for the little things, the things that make a difference culturally for our environment. We have a lot of fun with it."

Of course, like every business Zappos faces challenges: competitors are relentless, Wall Street is demanding, and customers must be served. But it's one business that has learned it must have fun cheering if it wants to grow.

But wait. This kind of shenanigan doesn't just prove lucrative for shoe stores . . .

THE THIRTY-EIGHT CHOCOLATE BARS

Gary E. McCullough, president and chief executive of the Career Education Corporation, learned the lesson of cheering in a powerful way during his days in fatigues.

As he has stated in a published interview, "The biggest lesson I learned early on in my tenure in the army is the importance of small gestures. As you become more senior, those small gestures and little things become sometimes more important than the grand ones. Little things like saying 'please' and 'thank you'—just the basic respect that people are due, or sending personal notes. I spend a lot of time sending notes."

McCullough recounted a time he was a platoon leader at Fort Bragg, North Carolina, and the division was on maneuvers in miserable weather. "It was February and it had been raining for about a week. The commanding general came around to review some of the platoons in the field. He went to one of my vehicle drivers and asked him what he thought of the exercise we were on. To which the young private said, 'Sir, it stinks.' I saw my short career flash before my eyes at that point."

When the general asked why, the private said: "There are people who think this is great weather for doing infantry operations. I personally think 75 and partly cloudy is better."

So the commanding general said, "What can I do to make it better for you?" And the private said, "Sir, I sure could use a Snickers bar." A few days later the division was still experiencing lousy weather when a box showed up for the private. The box was filled with thirty-eight Snickers bars, the number of people in McCullough's platoon. Inside was a handwritten note from the commanding general that said, "I can't do anything about the weather, but I hope this makes your day a bit brighter, and please share these with your buddies."

After that, McCullough said, the troops would have followed that general anywhere. It was a very small thing, and he didn't need to do it, but it impressed upon McCullough that small gestures are hugely important.

The way that we are treated on a daily basis by our colleagues and higher-ups, and the way that we treat them, has a great deal to do with both our individual success and with breakthrough performance by teams.

McCullough recounts another story that vividly portrays this point, about a woman named Rosemary who he worked with at Procter & Gamble. Rosemary was a cafeteria worker and had an uncanny ability to discern which employees were going to succeed at P&G and which ones would leave. "I remember, when I was almost a year into the organization, she told me I was going to be okay. But she also told me some of my classmates who weren't going to make it. And she was more accurate than HR."

McCullough asked her how she could make such good predictions. She said she could tell just by the way the new workers treated other people. She said: "You're going to drop the ball at some point, and I see that people like you and you treat them right. They're going to pick up the ball for you, and they're going to run, and they're going to score a touchdown for you. But if they don't like you, they're going to let that ball lie there and you're going to get in trouble."

HOW TO CHEER: A PRIMER

Cheering works. But how? One principle: cheering is motivating. And yet many organizations aim their motivation efforts at employees with a bias that a worker is moved by base emotions such as fear, greed, and ambition. Think about it. Many people go to work every day fearing that any minute they could be fired for messing up. Or they might receive an unexpected bonus or a raise for doing something terrific. Or they may have a promotion dangled in front of their eyes if they overperform for an extended period. These are, supposedly, why employees punch the clock.

Certainly these things contribute to motivation, but our research has shown that this approach is much too narrow, and can be counterproductive. For every worker who is clawing his way up the ladder, there is another who is perfectly happy fulfilling the job description and doesn't lose sleep over rank advancements. For every employee who is spurred to produce great results by fear, another simply becomes dumbstruck. For everyone who salivates over a possible year-end bonus, there is another who gets even more intrinsic satisfaction that goals are being accomplished.

One of the key problems with organizations appreciating the incredible value of recognition and cheering is that there is such a pervasive belief that employees fundamentally dislike work, and they are only putting in their time for the paycheck. The truth is that people find great satisfaction in feeling part of a team that is succeeding, and they are readily inclined to embrace a cheering culture.

Let's use a high school football game as an example.

Here is a cheering society in microcosm. Players are banging into each other, mostly oblivious to potential physical dangers. They aren't getting paid. Some of the team members play a lot and others sit on the bench a lot. Coaches yell and plan and pace. The coaches are paid, but not much. A band plays energetically. Not only are they unpaid, they have to pay for music lessons and uniforms. They get little respect. Nobody says, at the end of a successful game, "Great Sousa playing after the big touchdown." There are cheerleaders, pep and drill squads, stands full of students, teachers, and community members. Some adults have children on the field, others are former players, and others have simply self-identified as fans and are adopted onto the team as surrogates.

Why do they all do it? Sports are entertaining, that's one reason. It's fun and exciting, and—especially if your team wins—invigorating. But what about the sacrifices? Why do those people at a high school game, the players, coaches, bands, cheerleaders, and fans do it? They are seeking a bit of glory, and even if they aren't on the field spiking the ball after the winning touchdown, there is shared glory merely for being on the winning side. It's not true that they are doing it for the team, if by "team" we mean those with uniforms and helmets. Unless high schools have changed dramatically since we squeaked through, a nerdy fan isn't going to get much attention from the cool athletes no matter how hard he yells, "Go!" The response he's most likely to get from the quarterback is, "Go away." But the nerd gets something else, doesn't he? He gets a piece of it all.

This cheering impulse is strong in people in every culture and every country. It is not limited to classmates and neighbors. We cheer for people whom we have never met and are completely unlikely to ever meet. The World Series MVP isn't going to be your friend . . . and yet, after cheering for him throughout a tough baseball season, you feel, just a little bit, like you won the World Series too. There is something in it for you, and it has nothing to do with fear, greed, or ambition. Cheering is unifying, it creates an atmosphere of camaraderie and a willingness to accept each other and buoy one another. Cheering acknowledges that each person on the team, by himself, will be unsuccessful unless everyone works together in a balanced, concerted effort. Cheering praises those of high accomplishment, but it also supports those who are less talented if they try their best.

Any competitor knows the advantage of playing at home: it is cheering that creates a home field advantage. Those are soft and fuzzy emotional consequences. We admit it. In professional organizations it is logical to shy away from the touchy-feely. And yet, as people, we respond to them so strongly. Surely there is a way to bring the effective outcomes of cheering into our efforts as team members at work—surely.

Just look at some of the most respected companies in the world like Walmart, Home Depot, and Yum Brands—they literally cheer for each other in their meetings. Yes, it's the actual "Rah-rah" cheering. Can anyone argue it's not working for these brands?

This does not mean, though, that *all* cheering works. The way in which a manager cheers for employees and shows them recognition has a great deal to do with the results.

THE GUMBY EFFECT

One story that illustrates this is a case of good intentions that turned rotten at American Express. "We had a bad recognition moment," admits Robert Childs, the organization's senior vice president of human resources.

Childs says that through his twenty-five years supporting every line of business at American Express, the organization has always been a fan of recognition. But he adds that if the "cheering" isn't executed properly, it can have a demoralizing effect.

Childs was referring to a recognition idea tried years ago to reward employees who learned a new system in the business travel arena. "The system improved the speed and quality of bookings," he said "The whole theme around it was 'flexibility.' But we underestimated how much change was necessary to become more flexible."

New procedures were intensive and time consuming; still in traditional AmEx fashion, employees responded. And leaders wanted to appreciate their hard work with a reward. Great, right? It would be, except the chosen award was a Gumby doll. You know, since Gumby is flexible.

Childs cringes when he tells us, "Employees were quite upset. They had to change the way they worked. They had worked overtime to learn the new system. And their primary comment back to management was, 'You *have* to be kidding! A Gumby doll?' Instead of thanking them for their hard work in a meaningful way, we thanked them with a cheap, green, plastic doll."

While Gumby may have made a fun mascot for the project, it was hardly a fitting reward for this big an effort. And it was remembered. "Before each new system change that followed, people would ask, 'Am I going to get a Gumby for doing this?' We created a negative tradition—an ongoing joke that ended up becoming a huge hurdle to overcome."

Could AmEx turn the tables by cheering properly?

"It works wonders if you do it right," says Childs, and American Express has certainly implemented numerous positive experiences since learning from Gumby. "A great recognition practice was started by Ed Gilligan, our vice chair, when we were looking for more of a sales culture in Global Corporate Services."

If reps exceeded their sales target in a sustainable fashion, and were part of the top 3 percent of sales performers overall, they would be recognized as part of the President's Club. They would receive acknowledgment of the achievement on their business cards and letterhead, they would receive a symbolic award, and would be taken on a trip to a fabulous location.

Now such a club and such rewards might seem pretty typical in a sales organization. But American Express took this cheering and recognition to the next level by making it *personal* to each individual, and by making it *social*.

"We held a recognition event and had everyone attend," says Childs. "This way, everyone got a chance to see who the performers were. First we read statements about the accomplishments of each individual—and how those accomplishments impacted the goals of the team. We'd say, 'Mary Smith, from this region, has been with us so many years.' We'd recite that person's motto, and then we'd reveal how much she had achieved above target—10, 15 percent. But it's not just about numbers. We personalized each moment by telling the story of a relevant win—how a very specific deal impacted the company."

Very smart. American Express obviously knows how to publicly cheer for people. First they introduced specific metrics to pursue. They then recognized individual performance with incentives and levels of achievement. And finally they held a public ceremony to specifically cheer for the stellar performances. But what made the event truly memorable was bringing it home.

Says Childs, "Instead of just reading special comments about the person, we surprised them. We got video clips from family members and significant others. The family members talked about how proud they were of the person's achievements and how they understood now the long hours they worked. Small children were saying, 'I'm proud of you Daddy.' Employees were floored and emotional."

The extra effort American Express took to say "thank you" helped these high achievers understand that the company was committed to them and valued them. The fact that AmEx was cheering for its people created an even stronger connection to the organization in everyone in attendance.

American Express has since copied the recognition process in other areas of their business, and experienced fantastic feedback and results. We've seen few places where employees feel such loyalty. We can't count the number of people at AmEx who told us they "bleed blue."

In order to make sure you do recognition and cheering right, take a close look at the following five tips.

- **Keep It Positive:** Remembering a negative behavior and speaking about how much better a person has become is not constructive encouragement. During a cheer, mention only the positive—not the transformation.
- **Cheer Immediately:** The closer the cheer to the actual performance the better. It shows that you notice, and pay attention to the present.
- **Cheer Closely:** Most cheering comes in the form of recognition and appreciation, and that is best presented in a person's natural environment among peers (in their work location, not your office).
- **Cheer Great Work:** Cheering for specific behaviors that reinforce key values, goals, or even personal strengths will have the greatest impact on initiating repeat behaviors.
- **Share the Experience:** Often, cheering comes from the top down. However, the most meaningful recognition we see often comes from peers who best understand the circumstances surrounding the person's performance.

Ready to cheer? Let's say your team has just completed a project, hit a milestone, or accomplished something remarkable. Sure you've had some bumps along the way (what team wins every game during the season?), but all in all it was a success. Now's the time to celebrate, but what does that mean: a pizza party with the obligatory three-minute speech by the division vice president? Your team went all out in achieving the goal, so the celebrating shouldn't be half-hearted. The reward should match the effort.

Always plan events that recognize the effort—the long hours and above-and-beyond results, or even the quick wins. While planning, decide if you'll stay on-site, do a group lunch at a great restaurant, or invite everyone over to your house for a weekend barbecue. What will everyone enjoy? What will make this a special event?

During the celebration, avoid the urge to blanket thanks to everyone. Mention every team member's name and mention his or her contribution. Present each person with a handwritten note of thanks that specifically outlines the accomplishments you noticed. We all work harder when someone is paying attention to our efforts—why wouldn't your team?

Next, explain how the team and the organization has improved because of what they've done. And express excitement for the next challenge in front of you. Again, it's not a time to bring up mistakes learned or how we'll do things differently next time. Celebrations are positive. Save the reminders of missteps for private conversations.

Finally, present a memento of the accomplishment—something symbolic of the specific task. The more creative the memento, the more memorable it will be to those receiving it. The memorability factor is key. Symbolic reminders help us re-create the same energy the next time our team faces a hurdle.

Oh, and there is another thing to remember. Cheering doesn't mean presenting your teammates with the most obvious memento: cash. Unless you've got a fat budget, and are able to present members with checks for thousands of dollars, keep in mind that small amounts of money can actually be demotivating and leave employees thinking, "I worked every weekend and long into the night for months, and they think it's worth two hundred bucks?" Cash not only drains your slim account, it can hinder your team's productivity potential as well.

Here's a story to illustrate a better way.

Ned Lidvall, CEO of Friendly Ice Cream Corporation, and Cheryl Hutchinson, Friendly's senior human resources officer, told us how this 500-restaurant, 13,000-employee chain differentiates in their very crowded market.

Said Lidvall, "Every restaurant has a chicken Caesar salad. What's the difference? The culture of the company you are eating in. The way to win in a sea of sameness is to execute better. And that's not easy. You have to capture the hearts and heads of your people. You can't pay people to be creative and passionate. You must create a culture that inspires behaviors through recognition." Wouldn't you love to work for a CEO like that?

Hutchinson does. She helped her organization turn to recognition and cheering after an eye-opening employee survey in 2004, which showed a majority of workers did not understand the big picture, did not feel thanked for their efforts, and did not feel their manager cared about them. "It was an aha moment for us. As great as our product and service training was, we forgot to say thank you."

The executive team agreed a change was in order, but thought cash rewards would work best. Hutchinson put her foot down. "They thought cash was king. They said, 'Just give them cash or a $10 gift certificate.' I asked them if they still had a box of trophies in the attic from high school? Yep, everyone did. The items in those boxes tell a story. That's what recognition is. We want to have something that helps us remember our achievements."

Hutchinson then developed a recognition solution that connected to real business results—such as guest recovery and teamwork. And, no surprises here, the results have been outstanding, including a 40 point upswing in trust levels on their employee surveys. Good to have trust, sure. But the ripple was felt in the bottom line—stronger sales, higher guest counts, fewer guest complaints, and lower employee turnover.

"The cost savings from reduced turnover alone funds recognition at Friendly's," said the HR leader. "How can you afford not to have a recognition program? It accelerates business results."

Impressive, but we were curious whether the success that Friendly's experienced could be replicated in circumstances that weren't, well, as friendly. Would the idea of recognition deliver such business success in other industries? How about on other continents?

We asked executives at Pets at Home, the UK's largest pet store franchise, with more than 250 locations. On a continent where many senior leaders we've met deem ideas such as recognition and celebration too frivolous and "American," Pets at Home embraced the idea of appreciation in early 2009.

In addition to rolling out a recognition program and manager training to encourage great work, Pets at Home added a fun twist. They coined the tagline "Carrot Juice Powers Appreciation," and then got their hands on one of our four-foot-high Carrot mascots. The team renamed him Casper Carrot, and sent him on a year-long tour of their stores and distribution facilities. Colleagues were able to nominate employees who deserved recognition, and Casper spent a week in that person's location. The giant carrot kept a tour diary with him, and all the individuals he visited had their stories recorded. Pictures also were featured in the company's magazine, *Talking Pets*.

According to Ryan Cheyne, head of HR, "The Casper Carrot tour is a fun, high-profile way of keeping recognition at the top of our agenda. The results of our last colleague engagement survey were amazing. We had a 94 percent participation rate and our engagement index was 16 percentage points ahead of our benchmark group—made up of twenty-eight top UK retailers."

Cheyne also noted that the organization's overall annual employee turnover has dropped from 38.2 percent to 19 percent as a result of the focus on appreciating great work, saving the company millions of pounds in recruiting and training expenses.

Cheyne outlines the program: "We have carried out formal award presentations and informal celebrations, and we have sent congratulations cards. We applaud each other at our team meetings in recognition of individual great work, and we reward our teams as groups for their great work or performance. We have events to thank our teams where we go for meals out or on trips to theme parks, and even our quizzes with prizes bring teams closer."

When we asked Cheyne for the financial result on the organization from all these recognition efforts, his response was unequivocally upbeat: "During what has been a harsh global recession, Pets at Home has delivered sales and profit performance well ahead of the retail industry, regularly achieving double digit growth. Our colleague engagement levels have, without a doubt, contributed significantly to this success, and the way we are trying to reward and recognize our people is contributing to this engagement."

Andrew Blaney of Pets at Home in Scotland says there's been a contagious spirit emerging with all the recognition. "Each of our stores in Scotland now has a dedicated 'carrot patch,' a wall for all kinds of thank-you notes from customers, managers, and fellow colleagues. I have taken to writing thank-you notes early in the morning and posting them in individual lockers. Some make it to the carrot patch. Others, well, every now and then I catch a glimpse of the inside doors of lockers and see the notes I left posted there. That's the amazing thing about appreciation—people react in many different ways!"

A HEART AS BIG AS TEXAS

We discovered, in an unlikely location, a story that transcends mere teamwork. It is an unusually striking example of a leader who gets inspired, inspires others, and then everything comes together.

When you walk through the front doors of a Texas Roadhouse restaurant, you step back in time to the southern plains. This chain had 330 restaurants at year end 2009 and 40,000 employees system-wide, and was built to resemble a traditional roadhouse found throughout rural Texas, serving great food amid line dancing and country music. "We have a little giddy up and yee haw here," one store manager told us.

Your server smiles and says you can win a free appetizer if you can guess all the country stars on the wall. The appetizer is delicious. The ambiance, which includes peanuts on the floor and the smell of fresh bread from the bakery, is good family fun.

Company founder Kent Taylor opened the doors on his first restaurant in 1993 with a simple people-first philosophy: take care of your employees and they will take care of your guests. His focus on employee happiness was a departure from the conventional management wisdom at a time when competitors were focused solely on taking care of the guest.

In this remarkable culture, awards were created for meat cutters, bartenders, and line dancers. Other national promotions and contests combined for a lineup of recognition that was impressive, but disconnected.

"We began to realize we could create an exponentially better experience for our people by tying our programs together under one branded effort," said Dave Dodson, communications and recognition program director. "Now every program from early recognition to service awards to performance awards and national promotions fits under the 'Living Legends' theme in one easy-to-understand package."

Adds Taylor, "As your company grows you have to formalize the recognition because you can't go into every store and try to get people to get it."

To spread the word effectively, Dodson and other key recognition strategists have made regular trips to Carrot Culture workshops. "We've developed recognition programs in our company for many years, but it doesn't mean we're experts," he said. "Carrot training really helps us take our internal training to the next level. It always focuses on the most recent studies and best practices. And that's the point. You know the results organizations are generating through smart recognition programs are not just ideas. And that's exciting."

Learning to appreciate. Celebrating like family. It's an approach that recently earned Texas Roadhouse extra attention from the Wall Street press. In 2009 at the company's annual managing partner conference, CEO GJ Hart was invited on air by CNBC to discuss the company's decision to continue recognition practices. While media focus at the time was critical of using company resources to celebrate in a time of rampant economic cutbacks, Hart used the opportunity to create a rallying cry for Texas Roadhouse employees.

Read the words of service manager Wendy Ennis of the Clarksville, Indiana, restaurant, as she described to us Hart's appearance on the news network: "The whole interview was pretty incredible. Not only did GJ not apologize for celebrating his people's accomplishments, he said he wasn't sure it was enough. It's an honor to be a part of a company that's so committed to taking care of its people—especially now. At a time when most companies are saying, 'Don't love your people, don't do anything extra, just tighten the belt as much as you can,' it's almost as if our leadership does just the opposite. The message we get is,

'Take care of your people especially right now. Love your guests especially right now. Take care of your community especially right now.' And you know what? The guests tell us they can feel it too and they love it."

By continually engaging employees through a focused platform of consistent appreciation, Texas Roadhouse has inspired such employee commitment, not to mention stronger performance and customer loyalty, all of which contribute to better business results. "We have seen a double digit drop in turnover from just a year ago," says Dodson.

Other company metrics also speak to the success of Texas Roadhouse's approach to culture. In 2009, again during the recession, company earnings were at record levels.

For Hart the secret to Texas Roadhouse's success is no secret at all.

"For the life of me, I don't understand why if you claim your people are your biggest asset, then how can you not invest in them and expect a return?" he said. "It's a pretty simple equation that so many people just don't understand. And when you get tested on those challenges and those beliefs is when people really pay attention. Employees have very long memories. I'll invest in our people until the day I die. That's hopefully why we will continue to be successful."

The Texas Roadhouse story illustrates the power of cheering. There is potential in every team to be extraordinary.

Still, this story gets even better.

Once a cheering team is in place, it has the potential to become about something bigger than itself. That's what happened here.

ANDY'S OUTREACH

During our visits, GJ Hart told us the touching story of the Andy's Outreach Fund, an idea that illustrates the transformative power of cheering within an organization. "The genesis goes back to when I was in training at Texas Roadhouse, and I was working at a restaurant here in Louisville. I was going in there every day, just like anybody else, working hot prep, cold prep, doing the things that you do to learn the business the Texas Roadhouse way."

In that Louisville location was a fifty-year-old dishwasher, James Bryan, who was deaf. "I don't think he knew I was the incoming president. He was just so kind to everyone, including me. He was always there if I needed some help or if I needed some dishes cleaned. Whatever it was. He has always stuck in my brain as a neat guy.

"About six months after I was finished training, I was sitting in my office and Dee Shaughnessy, our head of HR, said that James had passed away. As a dishwasher he had struggled to provide for his family. And with five kids, a wife, and bills, there was no money for a burial."

Hart, founder Kent Taylor, and a group of executives paid out of their own pockets to bury James, but this event changed the CEO's thinking forever. Texas Roadhouse already had a means for charitable giving. What Hart realized was that it should be used not only to help outsiders, but their own people.

"Texas Roadhouse was an organization based on giving back to communities. And that meant taking care of your people in your restaurants. It hit me like a ton of bricks."

Hart introduced the idea at the company's annual managing partner conference. Someone suggested the idea of an auction to raise money. Vendors, executives, and even the GM of the hotel where the conference was held contributed items, and within five minutes the managers in attendance had donated $73,000 to help their own. At the next annual managing partner conference, a twenty-minute auction raised $410,000.

A volunteer board of directors was appointed, a process for applying for funds was put in place, and more than 90 percent of dishwashers, wait staff, meat cutters, and bartenders started giving what they could through payroll deduction. Andy's Outreach Fund was born. The name, by the way, is a nod to Andy the Armadillo who has long been Texas Roadhouse's mascot.

"We started to be able to help a lot more families," said Hart. "But our goal was to raise it. Instead of taking care of 50 percent of a problem, we wanted to take care of it 100 percent and really make this endure for a lifetime."

So Hart and Taylor, together with a group of investors and management team members, started kicking around an idea: A restaurant where substantially all of the profits would be donated to Andy's Outreach Fund. Not for a year or two, but forever. The group decided to ask employees for donations to build the restaurant, so there would be no debt to pay off.

Logan, Utah, was selected as the site based on projected economics and the town's tight-knit community. And indeed, Logan did get behind the idea. When word spread about the amazing concept, more than five thousand locals applied for the 165 open positions. In other words, more than 10 percent of the entire city wanted to work at this very unique Texas Roadhouse.

When the store opened in the fall of 2009 every one of the employees was donating out of his or her paycheck to Andy's.

We met Joel Barragan in Logan. He's the restaurant's managing partner and came on board a year and half before the facility opened. At first, he was planning simply for a career as a restaurant manager; that's stressful enough. But soon after his hiring he received a shock: "GJ gave me the story of James Bryan and what Andy's Outreach Fund meant to him. He was so passionate about it that he was tearing up. Then it hit me what this was. GJ looked at me and said, 'You've got forty thousand people counting on you. Can you handle it?' I thought for about a second and said, 'I'm a big guy, I've got big shoulders. I can handle it.'"

And Barragan and his team have not forgotten their charge. Today, as employees walk out of the serving area in the Logan restaurant they touch a picture of James Bryan that every employee has signed. "It's like touching the Notre Dame logo before going onto the field. We all touch it. We touch it every time we walk out of the service area," he said.

And in every one of their pre-shift meetings called "Alley Rallies," Barragan reinforces the purpose of the restaurant and updates the team on how much money has been raised for the cause. "We do everything possible to improve service levels and profitability," he said.

With the funding from the restaurant and employee donations, Andy's Outreach Fund is today able to assist thousands of employees with funerals, fires, natural disasters, abuse situations, medical issues, and many other crises that would otherwise render some employees hopeless and homeless.

Said Barragan, "There was a young woman who works at one of our restaurants who was involved in a car accident. She had to miss work and was worried about paying her medical bills. Andy's Outreach Fund cut her a check. I met her when I was traveling and she was sobbing. She couldn't believe a company would actually do this for her— that we cared that much about her to help with her medical bills. In most states, a server makes $2.13 an hour plus tips. If you are a single mom, a little help goes a long way."

He mentioned another story, that of an employee who had lost a child. "He had no money to pay for the funeral. Andy's stepped in to help. That story in particular touches my heart. I think about it all the time. I can't imagine what it would be like to lose your child and not have the resources to bury him or her. That's when I know we are making a difference in the world."

There are few companies in this economic climate that would consider opening a new franchise and giving the profits to help their own, but Texas Roadhouse is unique.

Says Kim Boerema, a regional market partner and a board member of Andy's Outreach Fund, "We reinvest millions in our company to benefit our shareholders every year, so it's a fair gesture to give back to our employees. As team members, we give from our hearts to those in need. And it takes all forty thousand of us to give so much."

Adds Dee Shaughnessy, Texas Roadhouse's director of care and concern (a great title by the way), "In the early years whenever a tragic event happened, we literally passed the hat and gave money, support, and often food to the ailing family. When we decided that we needed a fund that people could use during times of crisis, we found it was not a simple task."

It took Shaughnessy, Boerema, and their fellow board members two attempts to receive nonprofit status. To keep it the company pays for an administrator and legal services to ensure they are meeting all IRS requirements.

Says Shaughnessy, "Andy's Outreach Fund is Texas Roadhouse. It is our culture. It is about our people. And it recognizes that our people are our most important asset. We take care of our internal guests the same way that we care for our external guests—we give them legendary service."

Concludes Hart, "As a leader you can be up today, down tomorrow. But Andy's Outreach Fund is one thing that no one can take away. This is our legacy."

And the power of Andy's Outreach hasn't stopped there. Hart sits on the board of Thorntons—a convenience store chain spread through the midwestern United States. That company's CEO, Matt Thornton, heard Hart's story of Andy's Outreach. Matt and his family give generously every year to worthy causes, but adding a charitable fund to help their own was a different twist they loved.

So Thorntons introduced a "Champ Cares" program for team members who find themselves in tough straits. "We are a family of two thousand," said the CEO, "and for some of our members Thorntons is the only family they have.

There's no better way to show how much we care than to step in during a team member's time of need. It is just one more thing that makes Thorntons different and why people build long-term careers here."

Just a few months after launch, 100 percent of Thorntons corporate employees were donating, and participation in the stores was at one third (employees can access the fund whether they've donated or not). The goal was to raise $200,000 to kick off the fund: half from employees to be matched dollar for dollar by the corporation. But in those first few months the employees outdid expectations, donating 50 percent more than was expected—which meant over $300,000 was available to help.

Tony Harris, vice president of operations, added, "It is great to give to national charities, but when you give to help a co-worker, the guy that you work beside every day, that's true teamwork. We have the best customer service and profits in our industry, and it's because we know we can count on each other. We are in the people business, and what better way to show our commitment to each other than with a program like Champ Cares?"

Andy's Outreach Fund and Champ Cares intrigue us for a number of reasons. First and foremost, they are beautiful stories and a testament to the strength of showing people that we care about them, no matter where they may fall in the company hierarchy. We enjoyed hearing how the idea was developed over time in Texas Roadhouse, and then was adopted by another firm. But the thing that most impressed us about the stories is the employee buy-in to the idea, as is evidenced by the sheer number of employees donating to the foundations. It's an extraordinary fact considering most of these are restaurant or convenience store workers who are not highly paid, they are not coerced to donate, and most are contributing to a fund that they will never need to access. It isn't like a retirement savings plan. We believe the idea's success is a testament to a powerful desire among most people to be supportive of one another and to feel part of a larger whole.

FROM THE GROUND UP

We should add that it's much easier to cheer when recognition is orchestrated by such enlightened senior leadership as we've shown at Texas Roadhouse, Thorntons, Pets at Home, or Friendly's. But some organizations' leaders have yet to realize the financial and emotional benefits of encouraging great work through appreciation. Still, there is a great deal that a team leader, and any given member of a team, can do to get the momentum of cheering going.

We asked Zappos call center managers Maura Sullivan and Rob Siefker how they fostered the kind of team environment where people root for each other? The two gave us some inside examples. Sullivan said, "It goes back to our core values. It would be un-Zappos-like to not root for people. One team, one dream. You want your co-workers and colleagues to do well because then the team succeeds. And it's going to be reciprocated."

Siefker added, "And it's not something that we ever said, 'Hey everybody, you can't be jealous of other people's successes.' Our employees just do it on their own. It's amazing around here when somebody gets a new position or a promotion. The excitement level is huge. When we give promotions we find different ways of surprising them with the news. We make a big deal of people's successes."

For one recent promotion, said Siefker, the entire team went outside the building and hid. The person's manager grabbed the employee and asked to speak to him privately. They went out on the second-floor balcony. "When the manager told the person about the promotion, everybody jumped out from underneath the balcony and started screaming and cheering," laughed Siefker.

Not surprisingly, Zappos has also come up with a quirky version of recognition payouts. Siefker explains. "We have Zollars. They're like dollars—Zappos dollars you can redeem for merchandise that is really cool. You can earn them in a number of ways. You can do something great, something nice for a co-worker, or something nice for a customer."

It's just another way the company cheers for each other. You gotta give these guys their snaps. And you gotta open your mind a bit if you're still struggling with whether or not cheering is a game changer. We could ramble on forever about cheer—it is, of course, our favorite aspect of break-through teams, because it's so much fun and creates such measurable results. But if you're still in doubt, prove it to yourself. Pick someone on your team to cheer for right now. Revisit the five pointers above, and test it. It takes just a few minutes, but the impact can last for a lifetime.

Rooting for each other can change the world. That should cheer you up.

8

---

101 Ways to Bring
your Team Together

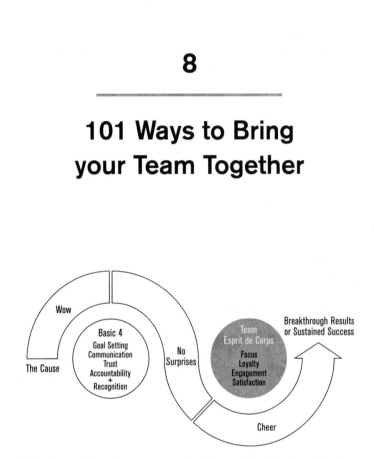

Wow, No Surprises, and Cheer: The Rule of 3 is a macro set of to-dos for building great teams. We now present you with a set of micro ideas: a list of 101 tried-and-tested ways to spark the camaraderie of greater esprit de corps among your teammates. Every idea was supplied to us by either a member of a breakthrough team or by the leader of a larger organization that has exceptional employee engagement.

Don't reject the list if a few seem out of character for your team. Some are applicable only to a large company, while others work best for smaller teams. Move through the list until you find something that will work for you. It's there.

You'll find the ideas fall into eleven areas of focus:

1. Shared experiences (training opportunities, outings, social events)
2. Shared symbols (organizational brands and emblems, team names, attire)
3. Shared challenges (projects, hurdles, milestones)
4. Shared rewards and recognition (team celebrations, individual rewards)
5. Personal balance (life outside of work)
6. Shared voice (values, goals, inside lingo)
7. Shared knowledge and skills (teaching, learning, developing)
8. Shared competitors (identifying rivals, nemesis, villains)
9. Shared fun (laughing, bonding)
10. Shared environment (office space, behaviors, traditions)
11. Shared relationships (familiarity, caring, interpersonal skills)

No matter the category, however, they all are about drawing closer together on the job (and sometimes off), and establishing a camaraderie that propels your group to new levels of achievement. Have fun (you'll see we have with the list).

It's time to start your revolution.

Shared experiences

1. Get your team together and ask them each to list three heroes and the characteristics they most admire about these people—whether Mahatma Gandhi (passion, commitment, integrity) or even the Green Lantern (the courage to be named after camping gear).

Use these lists as the jumping-off point for creating a team values statement together. *Great follow-up*: Put a life-size cardboard cutout of each teammate's hero in his or her office, and attach a sign that says, "My hero."

2. Hold a casual Breakfast Club before work once a month. Ask the CEO or another senior leader to speak informally to team members and answer questions face-to-face. Make it unique by serving something a little out there: after all, nothing says togetherness like chimichangas and orange juice.

3. Take photos of customers and use them to play "Name That Client" with your teammates at the start of your next staff meeting or send as an email attachment. Temporarily rename the conference room in the winning employee's name.

4. To give team members a little perspective on their work, take field trips to places where your products are used and talk to the people who use them.

5. Instead of sending employees to separate trainings each year, choose one and attend together. This may mean bringing a trainer to you rather than hitting the road, but it will do more to foster unity on a subject of importance to the group.

6. Mix things up by switching from a team newsletter to an audio CD or a podcast that employees can listen to on the way to and from work. Include industry news, market trends, messages from your CEO, benefit information, etc. Of course, don't forget to add a little levity. Put on a catchy tune, tell a funny story, or bookend a witty trivia question. You'll be surprised how a simple change of format can change the response to your communication. Plus, you can get all team members involved—sharing a rotating spotlight on the show.

Shared symbols

7. Adopt a team mascot. In our travels we've seen stuffed monkeys, rubber chickens, GI Joe dolls, purple buffalos, and many other interesting talismans. Once you've identified your mascot, plaster it everywhere: on T-shirts and awards, coffee mugs and pens. *Fun follow-up:* Once teammates have had time to acquire mascot attire, host a "Mascot Pride Day," where they are encouraged to wear their mascot gear to work.

8. Find an inexpensive but symbolic item to hand out as on-the-spot recognition. For Scott O'Neil at Madison Square Garden, it's a dime. Employees value the ten-cent pieces because they have meaning. When a basketball player assists a teammate in making a field goal, it's called a dime. O'Neil uses the dimes as symbols of teamwork, and employees proudly stack them on their cubicle shelves.

9. Encourage employees to take the team mascot on vacations and business trips and snap photos. Post them on the bulletin board and include them in team emails or a team blog.

10. Add your team mascot to employees' business cards when they reach a certain level of service, quality, efficiency, etc. These achievement-level logos make teammates part of an exclusive club.

11. Include your team mascot in silly videos that educate about company products or services. Who tunes out when a plush armadillo explains the complexities of discount pricing in a gravelly baritone? Show the videos each month at staff meetings or send them via email.

Shared challenges

12. *Saying* you are part of a team and *acting* like you are part of a team are different. Many people resist doing

certain jobs, even in a bind. Being willing to pitch in and do whatever is needed whenever it is needed goes a long way toward building trust among teammates. Pick a day to perform someone else's least favorite task to set the example.

13. To gain a better perspective on challenges team members face, set aside a day or two to work side by side with team members, doing what they do all day.

14. Create a self-fulfilling prophecy. In the middle of a stressful team assignment, greet fellow employees at the door first thing in the morning with a hot cup of gourmet coffee or fresh juice. Tell them that you are glad to see them and that you are convinced their project is going to be wildly successful—because *they* are working on it.

15. Play work bingo by filling in a square each time your team completes a task or has an achievement. When you've completed four in a row, the team wins a prize: a shiny, new Volvo! Or possibly a new team stapler: it's your call.

16. Have your team adopt a five-minute rule for help. In other words, if you are stuck on a problem, don't wait more than a handful of minutes before asking others for advice.

17. When your team is stymied by a challenge (i.e., "stapler" or "Volvo," etc.), meet in a quiet location and break into smaller groups. Give each a defined time frame for coming up with a solution. When time's up, gather together to listen to each proposal and reach a consensus for going forward.

18. Hang punching bags in the break room listing the current challenges to success. Encourage employees to "knock out" the barriers. *Variation:* Label the punching bags with competitor names.

Shared rewards and recognition

19. If your team members receive bonuses, attach a note to each check explaining what the individual did to earn it, and thanking him for his contribution. Deliver the bonus in person.

20. Ring a gong when your team wins a big deal.

21. At the end of each day, take a moment to gather the team and write down three things that went right. Getting in the habit of looking for the positives around you will pay dividends at the office, at home, and socially. It also gives you many things to recognize as a team.

22. When you're planning to recognize a team member, and you're not sure what to do, recruit the person's best friend at work to help. *Variation:* If you really want to recognize achievement, call the team member's significant other and ask for some ideas, and then invite the significant other to the office for the ceremony.

23. To come up with more ideas for building revolutionary camaraderie, ask friends outside of work about their best recognition experience and what made it so memorable.

24. When you spot a team member behind you in the cafeteria line, anonymously pay for their items and ask the cashier to tell them it's "payback" for all they do for the team.

25. Visit team members in their workspace on their service anniversaries each year, with balloons and a list of everything they've accomplished during the past twelve months. Make sure everyone in the room knows how glad you are that they joined the organization. *Great follow-up:* Arrange for the CEO or division leader to meet with the team member for just a few minutes. Face time with leadership is great way to help people move up in the organization.

26. Make a stellar performer the star of your next company video. Even better, use him or her in your next ad campaign. Employees and customers respond to real people; we can typically spot the fakes.

27. Encourage team members to put their names on the products they create. This includes reports, software, marketing plans, etc. Along with getting credit for their contributions, team members will take greater pride in their work and feel a heightened sense of accountability.

28. If you hear something good about someone, tell them! And tell everyone on your team.

29. Give each team member a stack of thank-you cards, and ask them to recognize co-workers when they see them furthering company values. *Variation:* Instead of cards, give team members a small budget to purchase team thank-you gifts.

30. The next time a teammate makes a mistake in an effort to move forward in unfamiliar territory . . . thank them. By rewarding the courage to try something new, you create a trusting environment where innovation can, and will, keep occurring.

31. Organize annual team contests to determine the highest-quality assembler, the salesperson with the most repeat business, etc. *Great follow-up:* Buy an ad and put the winners' names in the local newspaper.

32. Remember every employee's birthday with a card signed by the team. Write in the card a short list of the person's achievements during the past year. Read it together. It will be one gift she won't soon forget.

33. Kick off a staff meeting by asking each person to brag about one of their achievements from the previous seven days. At the next meeting, ask each person to brag about another person's achievement that they saw during the past week.

34. Want to Wow younger employees when they Wow you? Then call someone's mom and tell her how great her son or daughter is. Trust us, they'll love it.

35. Take responsibility for your own mistakes; but share the credit for your successes. *Fun follow-up:* Whenever you make a team-related presentation, make it a point to mention, by name, team members who helped—even if they just cheered for you.

36. Host a positive picket. When your team reaches a milestone, create a large banner saying "Congratulations to [Your Team Name]." Ask top leaders to stand outside holding the banner or placards as employees arrive to work. *Variation:* have the executives stand under the banner and cook breakfast for the group.

Personal balance

37. Here's one for home: Make a list of what motivates each member of your family. Is it a spa treatment? Tickets to a concert? A new game for the Wii? If you get stumped on a certain family member, make it a point to do something special with that person during the week—and really talk.

38. Promote your product and provide a benefit to team members by allowing them to send up to $50 of company products annually to friends and family.

39. Be a team outside of work: Form a band, create a basketball team, volunteer at a local charity, or train for a run together. *Variation:* Challenge your local nemesis to compete.

40. Another great way to bridge the gap between family and work: Celebrate the birthdays of team members' children. It doesn't have to be much, but an hour off on the big day will go miles toward creating a positive attitude for the team at home. For those without kids, allow them an hour off on the birthday of a pet.

41. When team members and their families suffer personal tragedies, be there to off-load work pressures by pitching in to finish assignments or covering shifts. If needed, offer additional time off and organize team members to help meet basic needs such as food, shelter, clothing, and child care.

42. Cut down on employee errands by arranging to bring in people they usually have to leave the office to visit, including financial planners, flu-shot providers, and even yoga instructors.

43. Establish core hours during which team members must be at work (i.e., 10:00 a.m. to 3:00 p.m.), but then allow them to set the rest of their schedule. You'll be amazed by how many employees appreciate the empowerment of choice and by the results they'll produce.

44. Create a caring community by allowing team members to give unused sick days to co-workers who need them.

45. Set up a team page on Facebook and encourage employees to become friends. *Great follow-up:* To learn more about each other, encourage employees to create and post funny lists such as, "25 Things You Didn't Know About Me, but Were Too Uninterested to Ask."

46. Take note of major life events for team members, such as births, college graduations, or anniversaries. Before the event, stop by to wish them luck. Or swing by afterwards to offer congratulations or sympathy, or just to see how things went.

47. When your team is under deadline pressure, bring in a concierge to offload home errands, like grocery shopping, picking up the dry cleaning, and putting gas in the car.

48. Ensure employees have the technology to access their office computers off-site. Periodically, declare

a "fuzzy slippers" day and let team members work from the comfort of home.

Shared voice

49. Now and then set a daily team goal that supports your company goals. Set it high enough to make everyone stretch. Post results on a big board. Host a quick award ceremony for the best performer of the hour, half day, and day. End the day with a celebratory pizza before quitting.

50. On Monday morning, gather team members for a stand-up meeting and ask each person to give a two-minute report on what they plan to accomplish during the week.

51. Organize a treasure hunt to reinforce team values or product knowledge. Start by hiding a container filled with inexpensive rewards for everyone somewhere in the office. Create clues that reference your values and goals, leading employees toward the prize. When you find the reward, take a moment to connect the exercise to the business.

52. To bring your mission statement to life in a different way, ask team members to interpret it in the form of a large mural on a wall at the office. *Variation:* Ask them to make interpretation videos and then hold a competition to see which is the best, the funniest, the most inspiring, etc.

53. Create large flow charts illustrating where your work fits in the bigger picture. Hang them in an area that gets lots of use. *Variation:* Hang photos of your customers using your products. Your team may do something as simple as put caps on glass cleaner bottles. But think about the bigger impact of what you do— keeping the windshields of family cars clean and safe. Obviously your work makes a big impact.

54. Come up with some fun slang that is exclusive to

your team. Like an inside joke, lingo understood only by teammates creates a sense of belonging. For example, "Don't mess with the gravy," meant a lot more to the early teams of KFC than just a recipe.

55. Take time to regularly describe to your team exactly what success looks like. Be specific; explain exactly how the end product will look, feel, even smell and taste—so they'll recognize it when they achieve it. Compare and contrast your team to the teams in this book.

56. Host a pop quiz about team values in a fun, game-show format, complete with prizes.

57. During staff meeting, compare your team values with corporate values. Identify similarities and differences and discuss reasons for the disparities. Then, what the heck, eat some pizza and blow root beer out of your noses.

Shared knowledge and skills

58. Create internal training manuals, employee handbooks, and other materials featuring team members as the experts. Compile your people's insights into a booklet that you can give to new hires on their first day.

59. One day a week, let employees work on a self-defined project. The only qualifier is that the project benefits the team.

60. Ask team members for their opinions and input on your most current project. Trusting their judgment and then acting on it is one of the greatest compliments you can give a person ("Your scarf brings out your eyes" being a close second).

61. Instead of leaving it up to HR or Training, invite a tenured team member to train a new hire in a job function at which that person excels. Explain in spe-

cific detail what qualifies the team member for this important mentoring assignment.

62. Invite everyone on the team to participate in the interview process for a new person by allowing them to interview for technical skills, personality, and cultural fit. Involving others demonstrates a high level of regard and trust—and it immediately shows you value each member's input.

63. Ask your teammates to imagine they are going away on sabbatical for six months and won't communicate with team members for the entire time. What are the most critical things they'd want team members to know about their jobs in their absence? How can you capture those ideas?

64. When a new person joins the team, give her an empty puzzle box with a note explaining how important each person is to the team's success. Ask team members to drop by periodically during the day with their piece of the puzzle. Have them explain what they do. Hold one piece until the end of the day, and deliver it to the employee just before quitting time, with the message that she is completing the picture, and you're glad she's part of your team. This idea can be enhanced if you can create a customized puzzle that depicts the company or team logo or mascot.

65. Give team members half an hour a day to read material that will help them contribute more to the team. Topics could include: leadership, teamwork, trade manuals, online industry sources, etc. *Variation:* When you discover a great business book, buy copies for team members and invite them to read it with you. *Fun follow-up:* Create a blog on your Intranet and ask team members to post relevant information from their reading for the group to share.

Shared competitors (identifying rivals, nemesis, villains)

66. Post financial results from each branch, store, or department, and encourage healthy rivalries.

67. Create a shared nemesis (the competition). Order some of their products and do a show and tell. Instead of criticizing, ask the team why some people would like the items.

68. Send team members out to check on the competition. If you're in retail, it's fun to give each person $50 to spend shopping your rivals. Ask everyone to report back at a specified time and share what you've learned. *Variation:* Visit a vendor that sells your product side by side with the competition and see what the sales people say about each. *Another variation:* Have employees anonymously visit your own company and evaluate your products and services. *Additional variation:* Dress up like a cowboy.

69. Create a softball, volleyball, or bowling league made up of teams from work. Friendly competition between departments pulls people together in a very positive way.

Shared fun

70. Working together with teammates, attempt to break a work record. Want to have fun after hours? Attempt to break a world record. And keep in mind that your "records" don't always need to be serious. One week, see if your team can outproduce everyone else. The next, see how many times you all can effectively insert the words "razzmatazz" or "hootenanny" into professional conversations. Get creative, and have fun.

71. Invite team members and their significant others to your house for a meal or barbecue. Welcoming teammates into your private space is one of the highest compliments you can give. ("You should consider this

an honor, Johnson. I don't typically allow employees to see me in the hot tub like this.")

72. Set up a coffee cart and ask a top executive to push it around to employee desks, serving gourmet brew. (If you can convince him or her to wear a frilly apron while doing it, send us pictures.)

73. Have a joke of the day. Invite employees and bosses to take turns in your stand-up meeting telling a joke—even if they are reading a printout from the Internet. *Variation:* If you have a team member who would rather present a word of the day and its definition, let her present it. And then challenge the entire team to use the word at least once that day in conversation.

74. On a Friday-afternoon break, buy cookies and get everyone together to make a Top Ten list of the funniest things that happened at the office that week. (Knowing you have to put together the list usually helps promote more fun.)

75. Set up a microwave, along with a casual table and chairs, outside your office. Whenever the mood hits, pop some popcorn and invite teammates to share it with you.

76. Have an executive dance off. In some companies we've visited, the highest ranking officials get up in front of the employees once a year to do their best "running man" or "Macarena." Everyone turns out for these events, except for the executive's humiliated children, understandably.

77. Pull a harmless prank on a fellow team member. In one IT department we visited, the developers rigged a ceiling tile to drop when a Nerf ball was thrown through a hoop. An unwitting victim was asked to make a hoop, when he was successful the ceiling opened and 140 ping-pong balls dropped on him. Much hilarity ensued.

78. Once a month, take a two-hour lunch together.

Choose the restaurant by placing team suggestions in a jar and pulling one out each time you go.

79. Hold a "Team Idol" competition on a series of Friday afternoons, with executives as judges and employee votes determining who goes on to the next level.

80. Celebrate offbeat holidays as a team such as Dragon-Slaying Day, National Carrot Day, Hockey Goalie Mask Day, etc. Or create your own team holidays to celebrate.

81. Rent a DVD of an inspirational team video and show it on a Friday afternoon complete with movie food such as popcorn, Junior Mints, and soda.

82. After work or at lunch, play an online computer game with team members—and mention the standings during a work meeting. It shows that you know how to play.

Shared environment

83. Move the break room to a more central location so people interact more. Add comfortable (and clean) couches and stock the fridge with free drinks and favorite employee snacks.

84. Ask team members to suggest ways to improve the work environment, and then really surprise everyone by acting on them—even if the suggestions are outlandish.

85. Create a sense of ownership by hanging unique and very prominent nameplates on teammate doors or cubicles. *Variation:* If your workplace is more industrial, you can create the same feeling by labeling team member tools, equipment, or nametags.

86. Let team members make their own rules. For instance, are there times or days when you will encourage toys in the office? Or does the team agree that you'll have no music blaring before 4:00 p.m., but will crank the tunes after hours?

87. Have a song of the day that blasts out at a set time in the afternoon. Try to make it describe what's going on that day, special events, your mood, current events, or just an upbeat song that fires people up. "Mustang Sally," "Born to Be Wild," or "Living on a Prayer" are a few songs we've heard blasted throughout organizations to great effect. (Warning: If you hear "Take This Job and Shove It" playing loudly you may want to track down the source.)

88. Come up with a unique way to greet visitors at your facility (give them a gift that relates to your business, have them wear a crown, blow noisemakers, etc.). Allow all team members to greet visitors in a unique way—it allows teams to show their pride.

89. Add a foosball or ping-pong table in the break room; then organize an ongoing double-elimination tournament during lunch. Award an embarrassingly large and obnoxious traveling bowling trophy to the winner. Remember: the team that plays together achieves together.

90. Eliminating executive perks, such as covered or reserved parking spaces and plush office space, sends the message that team members are valued as much as leadership.

Shared relationships

91. Bring something back from your next business trip for each team member. It doesn't have to be expensive; in this case, the thought really does count. Dried seaweed from Japan, beef jerky from Texas, or a Hershey bar from Pennsylvania means a lot, and gives your team members a glimpse into where you were.

92. Kindness counts at the office. If you don't believe us, just ask yourself: Would you do more to help someone you liked and who liked you, or someone who

is aloof and intimidating? Smile more today, say "thanks" and "please." It really does help.

93. Devote the first ten minutes of a staff meeting to building interpersonal relationships. A simple way to do this is to ask, "So, what did everyone do this weekend?" *Variation:* If you know someone on your team is focusing on an off-site goal, ask them about it. "How's your marathon training?" or "How is your volunteer work going at the food bank?" or "Is your puppy housebroken yet?"

94. Create a shared history by setting up recording equipment in a quiet area and encouraging employees to tell their best stories about work. Don't limit the type of story; collect them all, whether fun, sad, or inspiring. Include the stories in an audio CD, a book about the company, or in future company communications, accompanied by the names of the employees who told them.

95. Make a list of what you know about each person on your team. What do they do at work? What do they hang on their office walls? Do they have kids? If so, what are their names and how old are they? Then ask yourself: Which co-worker do I know the least about? Take time today to visit that person in her office and get to know her better.

96. Welcome new team members with style. Send each a welcome card before her first day, signed by every team member, expressing your excitement for her arrival. Have a small celebration her first day, explaining the qualities that set her apart from the other candidates.

97. When a new person joins your team, arrange for a different team member (or two) to stop by and invite him to lunch each day of the first week. This way, not only does the new guy get to know everyone individually, he also gets an overview of local eateries (including the ones to avoid).

98. Create a "survival" kit for a new employee, with fun items like a hand buzzer and lots of snacks. Take it by her desk on her first day and welcome her to the company.

99. To get a meeting started with a bang, have each employee come up with two truths about himself and one lie. The others must guess which is the lie.

100. Set up an employee-contribution fund to help team members in need. Pulling together to help each other out in difficult times builds camaraderie. *Great follow up:* Organize a committee to host periodic fundraisers to supplement the fund.

101. Learn to be an active listener. Practice eye contact. Take notes. Ask follow-up questions. The more you demonstrate that you can be trusted with concerns and ideas, the more your teammates will open up to you.

SIDELIGHT:

Orange Objections

If the process of creating a revolutionary team was a computer game, this section would be the "cheater's guide" that explains how to master it. In the following Q&As, we'll identify the most common teamwork challenges—identified through our consulting work, as well as focus groups and interviews—and give a few ideas for solutions. By the end, our hope is you'll be a revolutionary team expert, prepared to face whatever the corporate world sends your way.

OBJECTION: "Our team does not have a common grasp of our goals or what's required to reach our objectives."
Establishing a common vision and way forward is arguably the most challenging aspect of teamwork. That's

because each member comes to the table with a different concept of success and the best way to achieve it.

We recommend taking the team off-site for a half-day meeting. If you're the manager, this will be easy to schedule. If you're a team member, read along carefully—and use the following information to make a proposal to your manager that would include potential outcomes of such a meeting.

Kick the meeting off by immediately organizing people into smaller groups of three or four. (Don't let them choose their own groups; strategically form the teams to isolate bullying personalities.) Challenge the groups to quickly come up with a description of what success looks like. Set a time limit, and move the meeting along quickly, to avoid getting mired in the usual ruts.

When the time's up, get back together to see how the answers compare. Once you've come to a consensus on your single cause, break back into groups to brainstorm a pathway to it. Challenge teams to define specific goals, milestones, and a timeline. At the end of the predefined time, get back together again to discuss the different ideas. Remember that you don't have to choose just one plan; it's possible to integrate the best aspects of different strategies.

By this time, your teammates should be actively engaged in the planning process. And, now that you have a common cause and a path to success, it's time to make three commitments as a team. You can use the Rule of 3, or you can develop your own three. However, we strongly recommend the use of cheering as one of your commitments.

While you are on the topic of cheering, ask team members to define rewards, both personal and team, that would motivate them to move toward the goals. This should take the form of brainstorming with no answer eliminated. Outlining rewards is critical, because it appeals to everyone's "what's in it for me?" instinct.

If you have time, end the meeting by picking a team symbol or mascot. If you really want to go the extra mile, surprise team members during the next week by delivering T-shirts featuring the mascot, accompanied by personal notes expressing confidence that they can reach objectives together.

At the end of the meeting, you should have team members engaged in the goal, established path ownership, defined rewards, and created a team identity (plus, we hope, shared a great lunch and some laughs together).

OBJECTION: "We might want to be a breakthrough team, but our company is risk averse."

The term "breakthrough" can mean different things to different people. For companies that are more conservative, the idea can seem earthshaking; but it doesn't have to be. At Pepsi Beverages Company, for example, the breakthrough we described earlier was as simple as a slightly thinner bottle. Consumers hardly noticed a change, but it resulted in millions in savings and a better environment. If you think it will help, framing the discussion in terms of "superior results" puts most everyone at ease—and in a thought pattern of possibility.

We've also found that breakthrough teams in conservative organizations do best when they have a senior-level champion outside their team to argue their case, put things in perspective, and run interference. Most often, these high-level proponents continue to pull for the team even after it reaches its goal, helping to standardize changes across the organization. If your team doesn't have a champion, look for one. It's not about schmoozing the right executive. If your intentions are to create world-class results, the right executive will be thrilled to champion your cause.

OBJECTION: "We didn't have a say in our team goal, it came from corporate. And given our resources, time, and budget, it seems impossible."

One thing is certain—telling management what you *can't*

do is not going to fly. But that doesn't mean your team is destined to become a real-life *Dilbert* cartoon, either.

Instead we suggest taking to management a strong proposal of how—through a creative approach and willingness to stretch—you *can* meet the most critical and time-sensitive deliverables on your list. It's a "can do" statement instead of a "can't do" statement. Couple this with a strong case for a second phase, where lower-priority items are completed after the initial deadline. This proves that your team knows where to focus and prioritize.

The success of your proposal to extend some projects into a second phase hinges on demonstrating a revolutionary approach to achieving key items during Phase 1. Great teams are creative and innovative; they stretch themselves. So work your network, call in favors, and find a way. One national sales team we studied had a corporate goal to grow *and* an order to trim travel expenses by a third. Although it seemed impossible, the group found creative ways to couple delivery visits with sales calls, miraculously meeting both goals.

With initiative and hard work, you can turn this train wreck into a feather in your team's cap.

OBJECTION: "I'm a team leader and my team ignores me when I try to get them to do something."

This often happens when a person is promoted over former co-workers (and employees do not offer respect to the position) or when team members don't officially report to the team leader (creating a lack of accountability). But it can also occur when employees are required to participate in a team without having embraced the goal (a lack of buy-in).

If the problem is a lack of accountability, something a new team leader told us during our focus groups might help: "The toughest part of my job is to drive deliverables when someone doesn't report to me. I've learned that when

I have a report to senior leadership, I'll bring in the person who is responsible for that part on the project. I just had Alicia report on the new customer index to the executive team. Not to put them on the spot, but it does make them feel like partners."

If the problem is a lack of respect, you may want to seek out a leadership mentor who will help you to mentally and functionally make the move from co-worker to leader, so that you can act more assertively (not aggressive or dominant, but confident). Sometimes when we are promoted to leadership, we make the move in title, but not in demeanor.

Finally, if you discover that team members haven't embraced the goal, try bringing them more fully into the goal-setting process, as we discussed in an earlier question.

If after all this a member or two still resent being part of the team, it may be time to consider replacing them. We are amazed by the number of managers who inherit a team and assume they must live with it as is. As you replace individuals, remember that volunteers usually bring more enthusiasm to a team than those who are assigned to participate. And volunteers are more enthusiastic when they personally benefit from the experience, by learning a skill, being recognized, or networking.

OBJECTION: "We have some difficult personality types on our team. Some won't speak up, others want to dominate. How do we handle them?"

Making breakthrough decisions as a team requires robust discussion where everyone contributes. If you only hear the loudest voices, you risk moving forward based more on communication style than on substance.

To create a more controlled dialogue, make a habit of halting the spontaneous discussion of items after a predetermined time and "going around the table," specifically asking each team member what they think. Explain that during this solicitation of opinions, no interruption or feedback from other team members is allowed.

Creating a safe forum, where individuals are not challenged or attacked, may help reticent team members gain confidence. It also quiets dominant members long enough to get all the ideas on the table. And calling directly on disinterested team members forces them to participate. If, after going around the table a few times, you find your quiet team members need more encouragement, try assigning one of them to play "devil's advocate" on an idea.

A couple of additional tools for quieting loud voices so that a true exchange of information may take place come from Harvard Business Review's *Teams That Click*. For the "show off," who needs to hear himself talk and trumpets his own success, cut him off with a compliment as he pauses for breath, and then divert attention to another team member: "Ben, thanks for that detailed analysis of the third-quarter results. Scott, you had something to say?" For the "heckler" who interrupts every brainstorming session with criticism, respond by challenging him to come up with positive solutions, "You've told us what we can't do, Brian. What we need now are ideas on what is possible. Amy had a great idea."

Tools like these have a dual benefit of directing the discussion and controlling the use of time; skills your team members will greatly appreciate when meetings end on schedule.

OBJECTION: "How do we break up factions that form on our team?"

The short answer is to do it *quickly*. When factions are interfering with teamwork, time is of the essence. We've found that most managers waste an average of six months before they act to correct interpersonal issues. That's way too long.

Begin by immediately redistributing work and assignments, so the faction has less reason to gather. Next, examine what you are rewarding. If you change what is valued, you will change behavior. For instance, if you begin to publicly reward mentoring and positive attitudes, you'll get more of the same. Then, establish a common goal or even enemy outside the group, so people are not seeking a nemesis within the team. (You'll find some great ideas for doing this in our 101 ideas earlier in this chapter.)

Sometimes, nothing you do, short of replacing a team member, will help. One CEO we talked to tried everything to bring his divided executive team together, and got nowhere until he realized where the problems were originating: one rotten apple that was playing political games. With the removal of that person from that team, walls broke down and the team started to function as a cohesive group.

How do you know if you've got a toxic team member? A (nontoxic) team at Harvard Business School identified seven symptoms:

1. Frequently complains about and criticizes others in public.
2. Brings out the worst in other members.
3. Attacks people instead of criticizing the issues.
4. Talks in the hall but not in the room.
5. Constantly disagrees with everyone and everything.
6. Displays chronic discrepancies between public words and private actions.
7. Claims to understand his or her behavior but seems unable to change.

When an employee consistently demonstrates these traits, it's important to act decisively for the good of the team. If coaching doesn't work quickly, it may be time to replace the individual.

OBJECTION: "As a team we don't communicate effectively. We don't have discussions about tough issues, and problem team members are never dealt with."

It sounds like you've got an Orange Elephant in the room—maybe several. And until you face up to these hard issues, nothing is ever going to get done.

To get the flow of communication started, we suggest posing six penetrating questions to your team. We've found they work well to bring out issues that are holding teams back. Keep in mind, this is only a small list, meant to initiate the conversation, and answers aren't actually as important as the discussion itself.

1. Would you take blame for a team member? If so, when and why?
2. Would you work on a Saturday to fill in for a member of your group?
3. Do you have a best friend at work?
4. Are you emotionally committed to the team and what are your intentions?
5. What is the strongest skill and weakest skill of each team member?
6. Who has the best attitude on the team, and the worst attitude?

Once you've got team members talking, the goal should be to keep the dialogue going. The more you understand about the people you work with, the more prepared you will be to handle future Orange Elephants that attempt to muscle their way into your team.

OBJECTION: "We rarely celebrate successes as a team. I think management believes we get enough recognition in our paychecks."

Too many team members believe only management can provide recognition; and it's just not true. You can turn things around; cheering for each other is what the Orange Revolution is all about.

Starting today, make it a goal to find someone doing something right and verbally thank them. Do that each day. If you have a friend or two on your team that also values recognition, ask them to join in.

As more people catch the vision, invite them to commit to help you identify a milestone and plan a team celebration around it. Pool your resources, if necessary. As more people come on board, consider formalizing the recognition movement by inviting members to personally commit to the Basic 4 + Recognition. As a group, embrace the Rule of 3.

As the revolution gathers strength and achieves results, management will take notice of the improved esprit de corps—and of the people behind it.

OBJECTION: "We have big goals on our team, but we end up getting bogged down in day-to-day demands so that we never seem to reach our stretch goals that might make us revolutionary."

Yours is certainly not the only team to be stymied by this paradox. That's why so many revolutionary teams set apart one day a week for the sole pursuit of their "stretch goals." We understand that it's a leap of faith to devote 20 percent of the workweek to nonessential projects; but we've seen how, again and again, the innovative spirit generated by this commitment to pursuing revolutionary ideas spills over into the rest of the week; motivating team members to find ways to meet day-to-day demands in less time. If you build in time for "stretch goals," the results will come.

OBJECTION: "We've tried team-building activities before, but a lot of people roll their eyes or don't want to participate."

By definition, activities that create conflict and division do not qualify as team building; so it's important that you identify everyone's comfort level before diving in.

Start small, by maybe just offering popcorn and inviting people to chat. At some point, bring up your commitment to cheer for each other and discuss what types of team-building activities people would enjoy.

No matter what you end up doing, remember that it's important to explain the purpose of each team-building activity before you end up tying blindfolds on each other and falling backward into each other's arms (note: don't really do this). Understanding that there is a method to the madness might encourage reluctant team members to loosen up and give it a try.

OBJECTION: "If we give team members autonomy and empowerment, there will be no accountability. You need to have a manager in place who is accountable for performance."

Agreed. A manager does need to accept overall accountability. After all, somebody does have to assume the ultimate responsibility to report to corporate or the client. But a manager can't do all the work himself. How much more powerful a team is when team members are accountable for their personal deliverables *and* the overall success of the group. Remember what happened at Nucor Steel? It wasn't the manager who chased the lazy team member out, but the employees.

OBJECTION: "In our culture we don't celebrate heroes or revolutionary teams, but we also don't punish those who fall behind. Our leaders believe we are all in this together."

Your company reminds us of an organization we visited where the unofficial motto was, "All Our Ducks Are Swans." Everyone was valued, no matter what they contributed. While such thinking is certainly egalitarian, it usually breeds a culture of mediocrity. Where there is no reward for excellence, there's no reason to try.

It's this very type of environment, where no one else is

championing innovation, that revolutionary teams are so critical.

A leader in just such an organization told us he finally managed to lead his revolutionary team to achieve remarkable results. The company had no choice but to implement his group's changes corporatewide, but this leader was so exhausted by the fight that he couldn't revel in his victory. "It was like chopping down a tree with a hammer," he said of the experience. "It's good that we learned how to cheer for each other as a team, because no one else was doing it."

To maintain motivation and cohesion in your revolutionary team, it's critical for team members to individually commit to personal competency and for the team to embrace the Rule of 3. These guidelines will hold you together even in organizations determined to be mediocre.

OBJECTION: "Our team has tight deadlines, which means we don't have a lot of time for determining team rules, cheering, or honest conversations."

Fortunately, good engineers don't approach bridge building the way some business people approach team-building. Careful construction companies take time for evaluation (facing the unpleasant realities) and are willing to tear out the old structure and start from a new base (instead of just building on top of the old). The same applies in business. Revolutionary results are the result of a revolutionary approach.

It may take more time, even time outside the office, but it's just about impossible to achieve breakthrough results if you don't embrace each of the Rule of 3. You can't Wow if you don't commit to No Surprises and Cheer.

OBJECTION: "My team members are smart, and could be a revolutionary team, but they're afraid to make mistakes."

The only way to lessen the fear of making mistakes is to remove punishments. The Blue Angels have this down to a science. During debriefings, pilots are allowed to fess up to any mistake without fear of retribution. In other positive environments we've visited, mistakes are actually rewarded with bonuses or awards.

The only consequences in your team should be for failing to own up to issues or challenges. This type of environment encourages full disclosure, and that's exactly what you want.

OBJECTION: "We let a toxic team member go. Now, we've got to hire a replacement, and I'm afraid that we'll somehow end up with the same type of person."

In hiring, we see teams consistently falling into two traps. First is the team that thinks they are getting the biggest bang for their buck by hiring the person with the most impressive qualifications, experience, degrees, certificates, or number of pages in her résumé. But that's a mistake. While buying peanut butter in bulk is just fine (if you like peanut butter), it's no way to select a new teammate. Then there's the team who hires the same type of person over and over and over again, and wonders why they always gets the same disappointing results.

Instead, we recommend your team:

1. Look for competency and attitude, then train for skills.
2. Bring in individuals with different, but complementary, skill sets.
3. Make previous *team* experience a priority.
4. Look for empathy and integrity.

Numbers 2 and 4 on the list are a little tricky to get right. For example, companies seeking to enhance the diversity of their overwhelmingly homogeneous group will hire one employee outside of the norm. He or she then is held up as a sort of mascot for their broad-mindedness. But one token outlier will always be suppressed by the majority. Hiring for different but complementary skill sets must be a much broader and continuing undertaking.

Hiring for empathy is challenging, too. When we talk about empathy, we're describing the ability to listen to what other people have to say, identify the underlying organizational concern that person is addressing, and respond appropriately. People with empathy acknowledge other members' concerns before proceeding with their own agenda. They can handle it when they are corrected or their ideas are rejected.

Integrity involves doing what is best for the company, ahead of what is best for yourself. This means bringing up ideas and issues, even when they have the potential to negatively impact your team. It means keeping confidential issues to yourself. It means that you actually implement team decisions, instead of ignoring them. People with integrity do not pass the blame for decisions to someone else (i.e., "I didn't want to do it; it was Paul's idea"), or make decisions in a hallway after the meeting.

In short, hiring should always be viewed in the context of team interaction. You want to look for people with the ability to approach hard decisions and strong conflicting opinions in a way that builds esprit de corps.

OBJECTION: "My team was created by management and I think it's too large. What is the optimum size for a revolutionary team?"

Breakthrough teams are typically between five to nine members for more complicated projects, so you can make decisions with speed, and change direction as needed. However, with that said, much larger teams are certainly acceptable when your goal is simple and well defined. Realize that in larger groups it will become harder to win consensus, so the manager will have to play a stronger role. Another hint: For smaller teams an odd number of members is best because it eliminates ties in majority votes.

OBJECTION: "My team members are too wrapped up in their personal lives to make the commitments necessary to create revolutionary results."

We are all, at the end of every day, human. We have families, significant others, responsibilities, health issues, and personal dreams that may or may not be related to the goals of the work team. Acknowledge the other "teams" in your team members' lives and they'll respond by giving you better efforts. So often, organizations will attempt to become the first priority of a person's life—and, over time, the team members will start to disengage. Ask your teams what is important to them—which holidays mean the most, what their goals are outside of work, and so on. One team member may passionately value sitting down for dinner every night with his or her family while another may anxiously await the first snowfall in Montana every year to go skiing. If you value your team member's values, they'll value their role on the team.

9

The Company Is a Team: Creating a Revolutionary Corporate Culture

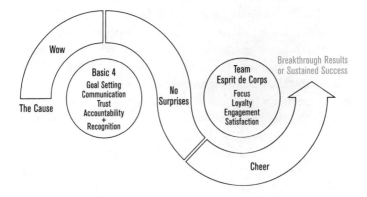

How does an organization instill any new culture systemwide? For many, it goes something like this: The big boss sends out a memo, a decree that henceforth all people in the kingdom will behave in such and such a manner, "Here is our new reason for being. We have a new motto: It's all about the Customer!"

The trouble is, such hollow slogans never work, and as employees notice more and more misalignment the mottos become counterproductive—undermining senior leadership.

Any organization truly wishing to create a winning culture needs to determine what initiatives would most engage its people. And there are the key words: engage and people. And few things are more engaging for your people than a commitment to work better as teammates.

Of course, there are many effective ways to inspire a culture that strengthens teams company-wide, driving either a series of one-time breakthrough results or overall sustained results. Here we focus on stories of several approaches taken, all with striking results.

A CULTURE CRISIS

We sat down with Alec Covington, president and CEO of Nash Finch Company, the second largest wholesale food distributor in the United States and a distributor to military commissaries and exchanges. The company's been around since 1885, and annual sales are about $5.5 billion. We wanted to talk to Covington because we were aware that he had created a team culture to turn around the company.

In 2006, when he arrived at Nash Finch, Covington walked into a storm of challenges. The company had been without a CEO for a number of months; there was a shareholder lawsuit pending. There was an informal SEC investigation. Customers were leaving. The cash flow of the company was declining. They were on the verge of technical default on their bank debt.

"Other than that, how were things?" we joked with Covington.

He laughed, then said that when he started everyone told him there was a financial crisis, but he disagreed.

"At first blush it did appear to be a company that was tipping over into some financial difficulties, but the balance sheet was still strong. What was really hindering the company was the culture. People weren't taking owner-ship. They weren't involved. They weren't engaged. They were afraid. I call it the 'bunker theory.' They were 'in the bunker' because historically if soldiers became visible, they would be wounded. The idea was to be in the silent major-ity that nobody knew existed. The real challenge was how do we get these people to care again, to want to win and participate on their teams? Because one person alone or a single management team can't do it."

Covington's financial plan for recovery began to work quickly, but he admits that the company wasn't really changing; they were just fixing the easy things. Ultimately, he decided that the real problem was employee engage-ment. So, through a survey, he asked employees to rate their attitudes and satisfaction with the company's management. As for his senior team, who Covington referred to as "the evangelists for all things culture," the survey revealed that employees were reacting to the leadership team positively. "They actually gave us pretty high marks," Covington said. "And we really had moved the needle when it came to integrity, respect, and results-driven attitudes, there's no question about that. But the employees gave us a failing grade in innovation, and celebration and fun. We knew we needed to dial in on those and ask our people to develop specific programs to help us improve in those areas and hold ourselves accountable for it.'"

Nash decided to create a team, aptly called the Culture Champions, specifically tasked with leading this charge. Employees would serve on this team part time, coming from departments all over the country, from food distribu-tion, and retail and military businesses, and include some of the most respected leaders and employees at Nash Finch.

Seeking the most honest feedback possible, Nash didn't give them a detailed top-down mandate about how they should conduct the process. Explaining how he tasked the team, he said, "Guys, we wish we had a template for how you should operate. What we have are problems, and we need your help, and we need you to work with our people. Get us more facts." The team conducted focus groups to gather specifics about opportunities in innovation and celebration and fun. And from that they constructed a path to improvement—organizing the areas of focus into levels of importance.

The leadership team at Nash Finch took the issue seriously. They decided that to truly change the culture of the organization, they needed to hone in on their shortcomings one at a time. Each year, they and the Culture Champions focused on just one of the problem issues that employees had highlighted. For instance, instead of rolling out a short-term initiative to encourage creativity, Covington wanted something larger. He wanted to change the hearts of his people and create a community that responded not only to the business, but to the larger world of need outside the company.

Then the CEO described to us what happened next. Covington found a hidden treasure already within the organization, the NFC (Nash Finch Company) Foundation. "The foundation itself had been around forever and it was an employee-managed team, yet it was kind of shoved underneath the rug. If you really want to bring out the best in people you've got to drive home that purpose-driven idea, but you also have to get them involved in doing something that they can feel good about. Go out to a food shelter and spend the day restocking shelves. When you go home that night, you know you did something that made a difference."

So here's where it got interesting. The NFC Foundation board, linked with the management group, started focusing on big community issues such as hunger. On the first Thursday night every month, a group from Nash Finch went to a nearby church to serve people in need. Over time they noticed that crowds they served were growing larger and ages were getting younger. The working poor were bringing their kids to get a decent meal in this church. Employees could feel the impact they were making. And they could feel themselves realizing the power of teamwork.

"We went down to the Dorothy Day Center in St. Paul with our management team," Covington reported. "We did an event to learn what it was like to be homeless. We talked to homeless people, let them mentor us. We asked how it happened, what's it like, what do you really need? When they were giving us a tour of the place we saw that the food shelter was barren."

Covington and his wife, Gail, personally donated a truckload of groceries, and they challenged the foundation to match that donation. The foundation matched the donation and the Nash Finch employees stepped up. The associates literally filled the company's lobby with food. They had seen firsthand how families were hurting. Said Covington, "We realized, if you really want to make Nash Finch people feel good, allow them to have a positive impact on somebody that needs it."

The fight against hunger for a food company was a true rallying cry. And since that experience, hunger is just one of the issues that Nash Finch employees have addressed. A program called Feeding Imagination provides books to underprivileged children. When that program started in 2007, Covington and Gail asked employees to donate just one used children's book. Covington told us, with a lump in his throat, "The following Friday employees brought in boxes and crates of books. Again the lobby was overflowing. It took Gail and some of the people from the marketing department two or three days just to get them all organized and shipped out. That's the kind of people who work here."

The culture of teamwork in Nash Finch's case has been enhanced by the desire of employees to make a difference in the community.

•   •   •

The upper management at Jumeirah Hotels and Resorts, a portfolio of eleven of the most luxurious and award-winning hotels in the world, took a different approach. A rallying point for their culture has become the chance for employees to be recognized for their outstanding contribution in their current role. These colleagues who are exceptional at what they do and act as ambassadors for the Jumeirah brand are named Colleagues of Exceptional Value (COEV).

"Working for this recognition motivates our colleagues and gives them a real challenge and sense of achievement when they are done," said Gerald Lawless, executive chairman of the Jumeirah Group.

Lawless obviously knows his people. The initiative has been a perfect fit for an organization that stresses individual creativity and initiative. Its success is borne out by the growing number of award winners each year, from nineteen in 2007 to twenty-eight in 2008, and to thirty-six in 2009. This number is only expected to grow, since coincidentally more than 60 percent of COEVs have been promoted to more senior positions after winning the honor.

Like most COEVs, one colleague, Basheer Veetil from Jumeirah Beach Hotel, can't say enough about his experience with Jumeirah. Upon receiving his award, he was tapped to be a Jumeirah ambassador at a travel and hospitality trade show in Germany. Besides being thrilled by the opportunity to travel, he was honored by the chance to represent his company.

"The pride and excitement that Basheer showed was just amazing," said Lawless. "And that feeling of loyalty and energy has not faded upon return. Basheer 'oozes' passion and enthusiasm for our brand."

So do the other COEVs. But even among such energetic promoters, Veetil's commitment to his guests stands out. He's the only hotel employee we've ever met who has had a racehorse named after him, in honor of the unbeatable service he provided. Not that the other COEVs aren't trying. "As a COEV, I will continue to inspire my colleagues to make a difference in this company," pledges employee Girald Manuel.

What Manuel and Veetil are essentially doing is declaring their intention to be opinion leaders in their organizations. That's gold, because it means that these COEVs may indeed become leaders among their peers; not because they were "appointed" to the job by leadership, but because they have chosen to rise to this level of dedication.

We saw this type of culture charge from leadership inside many of the organizations we studied. Certainly companies such as Home Depot, Southwest Airlines, and Starbucks use their culture brands as a point of market differentiation. And the list of companies that understand the impact culture plays is steadily growing. Over the next few pages we present a basic blueprint for building a team culture that managers can follow in any organization. Like any movement, it can start small—with one team—and grow exponentially.

HIRE FOR COMPETENCE *AND* CULTURE

We've talked about the importance of personal competence; and if you ask managers, most will admit they hire for that quality, first and foremost. But many great leaders hire for culture first, and competence second.

Says Arte Nathan, a legend in the human resources profession, "Great teams and great companies are built when great attitudes are combined—when people understand that they're part of a bigger vision, and they support and hold one another accountable to achieve the bigger vision. Great skills with bad attitudes will get you nowhere."

Nathan should know. In his job, he hires up to ten thousand employees at a time. In a matter of a few months, he has to build an organization from the ground up, get a multitude of workers to function as effective teams, and be ready to provide the highest possible level of service to discerning customers who expect perfection from the first day of operation. You see, for over two decades Nathan has overseen human resources for Steve Wynn's casino and resort companies.

"The Wynn Resort & Casino complex has a reputation," says Nathan. "That reputation can only be achieved if the right teams are in place. To run it, we once hired over ten thousand people, with positions that ran the gamut—cooks, housekeeping, maintenance, and casino staff, all the way to senior executives. We hired them all in less than five months."

To accomplish this task, more than 125,000 people were screened, tracked, and managed. "The goal was for every applicant who left the Wynn Casino recruitment experience to feel like they were a guest," says Nathan. "We wanted to meet and get to know each and every person who walked through that door. Otherwise, how would we know if there was the right attitude and chemistry?" Obviously, that's an impressive commitment to hiring for culture.

And yet an example of skills/attitudes out of balance can be found within some modern symphony orchestras. Reacting to criticism about unfair hiring practices, many orchestras abandoned traditional audition methods. Instead, candidates had to play their audition pieces behind a screen. Those listening could not see the musicians, which meant they didn't know their names, ages, gender, or anything about their experience. Finally, after playing several rounds of auditions, a musician would be offered the job, and the screen was removed. Theoretically, it was the most fair approach to hiring. And it did eliminate prejudices that had become all too common—after all, their job was just to create beautiful music, right? Well, there were problems with this approach.

An orchestra is an elaborate team. By hiring solely for competence and ignoring the player's ability to play well with others, musical organizations inadvertently created gangs of talented, tenured, unionized prima donnas. In fact, today many orchestras conduct only the first round or two of auditions behind a screen, and then allow the finalists to play with their potential peers, gauging how well they play with section mates, not just by themselves.

With the screen or competence-only approach, an organization must assume that each team member will buy into the common values. That is unrealistic. To determine whether team members really believe in the organization's purposes, the candidates have to show that they are fully supportive of the specific culture of the entity. That process requires time and face-to-face interaction.

GIVE POWER TO THE PEOPLE

As we've studied effective teams over the past two decades, and as we've conducted a year's worth of interviews for this book, a common theme emerged: breakthrough team members can make their own decisions, on the spot. A wise manager told us, "Success doesn't come from being a powerful leader, it's from leading a powerful team."

Great teams may start with competent employees who commit to rules of conduct, but their performance really takes off when they are trusted by their leaders to make decisions that affect their work and their customers. One senior leader we heard from in a focus group had seen the light. She was blunt when she said, "Over the last few years we've made a transition from asking our employees to check their brains at the door to actively asking our employees for their ideas."

As we've met with new teams just starting out, it's our experience that morale is typically high. It's very high, in fact. In the beginning, there is a belief among the members that the task they have been given is important. They feel pride—knowing they're trusted. But that trust is immediately undermined when leadership holds the reins too tightly.

Here's one example that impressed us as we studied a team within a large utility. Tasked by management, a group of ten people from marketing, sales, customer relations, and construction gathered a few times a week to address a potentially sticky situation: natural gas lines in an older area of town were aging and incurring a higher than normal incidence of leaks. The utility was about to send out "sniffer" trucks to identify areas with small traces of gas in the atmosphere. Those small traces of gas indicate a larger leak is looming—a potentially dangerous situation. So, obviously, when the small leaks were identified and mapped, construction crews would be dispatched to fix the problem areas.

Simple enough? You'd think so, wouldn't you? But there were some issues.

Senior management had learned that they would get a flood of calls from concerned residents if these space-age sniffer trucks began crawling up and down streets or crews started ripping up the tarmac. They asked the team that had been meeting to discuss the problem to determine, first, if they should let the local residents know what the crews were doing, or was it best to continue a business-as-usual silence? Next, they wondered, if they did communicate, how could they do so in a way that avoided alarming anyone?

The new team met. They quickly and unanimously agreed that the company's reputation would be enhanced by openness and honesty, and decided to communicate to the public about their "spaceships." They then debated the options and decided on direct mail to the affected ZIP codes: a campaign of three flyers—one before the sniffer trucks came, one during the construction phase asking for patience, and one after, assuring the residents that all was well.

The two marketing members on the team developed a choice of messages—ranging from serious to lighthearted—

and the group decided to test the flyers with focus groups made up of local residents. They knew their budget was tight, so they opted to conduct just two such sessions.

While hosting the focus groups, the marketing team learned that the residents were actually pleased to be informed about the work the utility would do. But then something unexpected happened. In both groups, residents said that they would ignore all the messages except the lighthearted ones. They talked about how those flyers portrayed confidence—that the utility had a good grasp on the issue, was interested in the public's safety, and wanted to get the message across in a way that people would remember.

The lighthearted flyers tested through the roof for memorability, impact, and clarity. Both groups said that if they received the fun messages, they would have a strongly favorable opinion of the utility and its workers. The team members were ecstatic. They had their solution.

The team leader reported the good news to the company president. The next day she returned to the team with the president's feedback. And, as luck would have it, we were there to hear the news as well. We have changed the name of the CEO, but this is the dialogue.

Team leader: *"We've had a change in plans—a slight one. We're going to go with just two messages, one before and then one after."*

Customer relations rep: *"Whoa. What happened? We went from three to two? No!"*

Team leader: *"Stan [company president] thought it would save money to just send out two cards. He thought three was overkill."*

Marketing rep: *"Five would be overkill. How is three overkill?"*

The argument continued for a few more minutes. The team leader expressed sympathy at the team's frustration, but admitted there was nothing she could do. Stan had spoken. She then added:

> **Team leader:** *"I might as well tell you, too, that Stan didn't like the headlines—the fun ones. He wants us to go with simple messages, nothing that could be construed as unprofessional."*
>
> **Sales rep:** *"But Stan wasn't in the focus group. He didn't see those people. They weren't even paying attention until we showed those things. You saw their faces. You know they lit up."*
>
> **Team leader:** *"I don't know what to tell you. Stan said he had a gut feeling about them. They didn't sit right with him."*

And that was that. Do you think anyone associated with this team ever volunteered to be on another cross-functional team? Are you kidding? This demonstration of command-and-control behavior essentially killed innovation and empowerment.

In fact, one of the negative associations with the word team comes from agricultural farming. A team of animals (oxen, horses, etc.) are harnessed together to accomplish something that a single animal could not. On the farm, a team is a group that is not asked to think but merely do. And there is a reason for that. Without direction, a horse wouldn't wake up each morning with the ability to add productively to the farm. Yet horses do run fastest when untethered. Unlike our four-footed friends, most human teams simply don't work at their full potential in an environment of harnessed direction. We need certain freedoms. Certainly in a creative sphere, team members have to have the expectation that they are in control of their actions. We can work for the greater good—we thrive doing that, in fact—but we must have a sense of self-determination.

KEEP SCORE

Nothing convinces employees, senior management, and others of the power of teamwork like results. Want to get support for this idea, then show the impact on innovation, camaraderie, and engagement.

We've all become jaded by business-speak. There's always a new buzzword that promises terrific results if a company will only. . . . It's almost becoming like the language of dieting. Try this new supplement and all your worries will be gone. But instinctively we trust old-school values: support, innovation, friendship, loyalty, dedication, teamwork. The best way to convince others that a team is valuable is to offer proof. For example, when people are engaged on their team they don't quit, they give more effort, they serve our clients better. That saves money, drives profits, and paves the way for further progress. Old school.

We encountered this firsthand when we started talking about recognition (in Carrot form) years ago. Intuitively, many business people knew employees who received appreciation would outperform their peers, but they needed the empirical evidence of our research. When they discovered that in addition to being fun and the right thing to do for another human being that recognition was actually an incredibly savvy business move, most were hooked. It's that simple. Use results to solidify the progress you are making with your team efforts, particularly in culture building. These are the kinds of facts that spread quickly through an organization and become the standard way of acting.

ACTIVELY BUILD ESPRIT DE CORPS

It's funny how organizations fight the idea that work should and must include a little levity. It boils down to these questions: Do you like your job? Do you like the people you work with? If the answers are yes, you're likely to work harder and smarter than if the answers are no. So it's in the best interest of everyone involved to create an atmosphere that allows all members of the team to feel camaraderie at work.

With that said, build a fun, engaging culture from a new hire's first day on the job. Celebrate individual birthdays (not in the convenient, impersonal once-a-month catchall). Have fun in the December holidays. Dress up at Halloween. Heck, even celebrate Arbor Day. Start a tradition of acknowledging the happiest person of the week in each staff meeting. Help employees bond to their teams and the overall organization. (Look again at the 101 ideas in chapter 8.)

Some organizations try to skirt the issue of esprit de corps by bribing their employees one way or another. That's what the word "compensation" is all about. They compensate for the fact that the worker isn't really happy or engaged but he'll stay if he's paid. But, as we've explored earlier, motivation doesn't work that way. The theory that pay drives us is a myth. Ultimately, if she's disengaged, an employee will either move elsewhere or tune out on the job. Even if she receives regular annual bonuses, she'll look for a bigger bonus someplace else. The content, engaged person, on the other hand, knows a good thing when he sees it. He'll give you his all. And that's money in the bank.

RECOGNIZE, RECOGNIZE, RECOGNIZE.

By their nature, recognition and rewards bring teams closer together. Develop and implement a plan to recognize individuals and teams and you'll also not only have built-in excuses for bonding, you'll spur greater achievements. Managers recognize employees. Employees recognize co-workers and even their managers. Everyone recognizes the teams that drive your business forward.

"I remember working with the housekeeping department at the Golden Nugget," Arte Nathan recalls. "Turnover was horrible—at around 300 percent. And even though we knew that it was high, and that it was a huge cost to the organization, a solution seemed elusive. Then, one day, I approached a departing employee. The employee was leaving the Nugget to work in the exact position at a different property. They would be basically doing the same exact job, for the same pay. And I wanted to know why they would leave. Was it poor management? Was it poor communication? Was there a working condition I wasn't aware of?"

"Communication is fine," said the employee. "Working conditions are fine. The people are nice. I like the property. But every time we have a meeting our failures are the focus. Even when we improve, the only aspects of our work that are discussed are the things we could have done better."

"It was one of those aha moments," said Nathan. "Immediately, I knew we could do something about the problem. That's when I learned the value of recognition."

Nathan implemented a recognition program where employees would earn points for everything they did right. They would earn extra if they went above and beyond. And the results of his program initiated a change that reaped unprecedented success.

"Turnover dropped from 300 to 60 percent in just six months," said Nathan. "And it dropped to 10 percent after a year. Plus, productivity rose. It was a huge learning experience for me. People became engaged in the organization like we hadn't witnessed before. They supported and challenged each other. And we saw teamwork like we couldn't have imagined."

Let's repeat that. Turnover went from 300 percent to just 10 percent in twelve months. Productivity went through the roof. Those kinds of results were impossible for this savvy executive to ignore—for anyone to ignore.

It's these types of stories that are fantastic lessons for all of us. As we've studied the process by which managers and team members were successful at encouraging and nurturing the growth of a spirit of teamwork, we have also identified key insights about the best role for the manager and senior leader in the creation of esprit de corps corporate-wide:

1. **Allow it:** If you see it happening, give permission to allow it to grow. Keep in mind that you may think a few mavericks are joining forces to create trouble. But with like-minded counterparts, has-been trouble-makers can become breakthrough team leaders.

2. **Train it:** Don't assume any of this comes naturally. Create development opportunities for people to understand how to find and build their breakthrough teams. Teach them how to create opportunities for honest elephant-in-the-room discussions—giving people a chance to discover others who may share passions, perceptions, etc.

3. **Find it:** Look for teams operating at outlier levels or those with the potential to do so and foster appropriate situations and conditions for their success. Your job is to realize the breakthrough team exists and allow it to exist—not to control it.

4. **Reward it:** Show the teams that you notice their shared vision and passion, and that you appreciate it. Don't wait for a final outcome to say thanks, but reward every step toward success along the way. Frequent recognition will only make the team achieve more.

5. **Promote and profile it:** Realize that all employees want to be part of a great team. Promote members of outstanding teams, and communicate how their commitment to each other boosted the organization as a whole. Let others learn from their success.

10

An Orange Life:
A How-To Guide for Living

Every spring, as predictably as the swallows returning to Capistrano, hopeful young kids pack grassy fields for club soccer tryouts all across America. They give-and-go and banana kick their hearts out trying to catch a coach's eye and earn a spot on a coveted traveling club team—a big leap up from the relaxed world of recreational soccer.

Just as inevitable as the arrival of spring, a large group of kids, in grass-stained knee socks, will go home disappointed from these tryouts. There are tears and hugs, and then that's the end of it. Life goes on, minus the cleats and shin guards.

But in the spring of 2009 things went very differently in one western town. It began when the father of one of these rejected eleven-year-olds petitioned the local soccer league to create a second Double A team for girls who had been told they weren't good enough for club ball. He persisted long enough that the league finally relented, as long as he coached.

So he took the players no one else wanted, calling them one by one to give them the good news that they would indeed play. At the first practice, surveying his ragtag group, it didn't take long for coach Pat Poyfair to realize why these girls hadn't made the cut. Some had never played soccer before, others lacked the height, speed, coordination, or courage to play at this accelerated level. For a moment, Coach Poyfair wondered what in the world he was thinking, trying to compete with this ragtag bunch in the toughest league in the state.

But the coach didn't throw in his towel and whistle right away, especially since his daughter was now the starting fullback. He had an idea. With little hope of much success anyway, his plan was to approach soccer as he would a staff meeting at work: seeing Orange. He would teach them to cheer for each other, so at least their experience would be positive.

So when on the first scrimmage one young girl chased down the ball ahead of the pack and kicked with all her might . . . straight into the wrong goal, he took a deep breath, smiled, and recognized her speed and fearless determination. When a player's attempted header missed her forehead and gave her a bloody nose, he dug out a towel and praised her enthusiasm for all to hear.

The girls watched and learned—and not just about soccer. With Coach Poyfair's encouragement, they stopped finding reasons to blame their teammates for their inadequacies, and instead actively sought out reasons to praise each other. Coach completed the circle by praising them when they praised other girls. In this hopeful, happy place, bursting with esprit de corps, the team—named the Arsenal Strikers—headed to their first three-game tournament.

As luck would have it, in the first game of the tournament they drew the defending state champion at the Triple A level for their age group: The best eleven- and twelve-year-old girls in the state. For those of you who don't follow minor league girls' soccer, Triple A is a cream-of-the-crop team. Double A is the next level down. In the total scheme of things, the Arsenal Strikers were the basement of competitive soccer.

Predictably, it was a massacre; the final score of that first game was a devastating 12–0. "They were crying," he said. "I didn't know what to do." So Coach Poyfair gathered the team around and asked them to take a knee. Instead of complaining, he rewarded their top performer—a girl who had run her heart out at midfield—with a Garrett the Carrot stuffed toy. (Those of you who are familiar with our "Carrot" series of books on employee recognition will recognize Garrett as our mascot.) As part of the presentation, amid loud sniffles, Coach Poyfair described exactly what the girl had done to Wow. "Hailey never gave up," he said. "And that's what we do on the Strikers. We keep running when everyone else walks and one day soon we are going to win because of that." The sniffles slowed and finally some smiles emerged as Hailey was congratulated.

In the next game the girls played another Triple A team and lost again, but this time by only three goals. Once more, the coach followed the game with a recognition ceremony to acknowledge the star of the match. This time the team nominated a few girls and members voted who should receive the Carrot. They chose the goalie Emily who had not only stopped a dozen shots, wowing her teammates, but had spent the entire game calling out encouragement to her fellow players up the field.

By the third game of the preseason tournament, the girls had a pretty good idea of what it might take to wow each other and the coach. They would simply run their hearts out, be sure to get back on defense to keep the ball out of the net, and would constantly encourage each other. And a small miracle happened. Despite playing a Triple A competitor, they tied. When the final whistle blew the girls jumped up and down at midfield like they'd won the World Cup.

The girls played a few more preseason games, and after each Coach Poyfair awarded a Carrot to the top performer. The girls began to tie Garretts to their backpacks and display them at school and on the way to the pitch. They were all turning Orange.

And with that color change, it didn't take long for the girls to begin holding their own on the field. Coach Poyfair saw that as success in and of itself. But there was more to come—a whole lot more.

On the first game of the regular season in the Double A league, the girls, pitted against the very Double A team that wouldn't take them, played their competitors to a 1–1 draw before losing in the last seconds 2–1. Standing around in a circle on the field after the game, the coach could tell that something had changed. These weren't the same nervous, unsure girls that had showed up on the field the first day of practice. They were starting to believe in themselves and the praise and recognition they were sharing, and they were ready to prove what they could do.

That's when the magic really happened. Following that first regular season loss, the Strikers went on to win eight games in a row. And they didn't just squeak by competitors; they won by two, three, four, and five goal margins against teams considered to have superior talent. Armed with the confidence that when they wowed someone would cheer for them, they got better every game.

As it happened, the Strikers finished the regular season playing the league's best team. This was an established group of girls who had played together for five years. It was a team that had not only remained unbeaten all year, they hadn't even been scored on. But Coach Poyfair's daughter Kristen put one in the top corner of their opponent's net late in the first half. Despite a valiant fight, they eventually lost 2–1 in overtime.

But it didn't matter a bit. More important than proving their soccer skills to the rest of the league, the girls had proved to themselves that they were a team. There were no tears (well, no *sad* tears) at the final post-game Carrot presentation, only smiles.

In the end, out of the fifteen teams in the Double A league, the Strikers finished third—well ahead of the team that didn't want them. The Strikers became celebrities at school. Everyone wanted to know their secret.

"I've had coaches from our league and other leagues call me to figure out how we did it," said Coach Poyfair. "I told them it was all about the power of Orange, about wowing each other and cheering for each other." Some believe him, others are doubtful. But in the end, it doesn't matter what anyone else thinks. For this coach, leading the Strikers was a tremendous validation of the power of Orange.

But wait a minute. Let's take a closer look at it. The idea of cheering is something that is highly effective in the workplace. And yet we also know that it works in our nonwork life. The funny thing is how often we keep the two separate, to the detriment of both. Each of us, to one degree or another, has an imaginary line that differentiates our work persona from who we are in our personal lives. For eight, nine, or ten hours a day, we work with colleagues, set goals together, communicate back and forth, and recognize each other's accomplishments. When evening comes, we turn off the lights and head home, leaving our best relationship tools behind, at the office. The very skills that we develop at work that could improve our personal lives are repressed. We're like Peter Parker/Spiderman or Diana Prince/Wonder Woman, and unfortunately, a dual life can wear anyone, even a superhero, down.

Real people face the same challenges. Liz is an outgoing, witty, and personable teammate. Her employees and others simply *must* seek her out each morning to hear the latest buzz, get some advice on their projects, and sample some of her contagious energy. She is tolerant of mistakes and encourages the development of those around her. Her work style is laced with open communication, stellar results, and a healthy dose of cheer for her workmates. She sets a great tone for the whole office.

But at home Liz is a total opposite. She is apathetic or even negative. She belittles her husband and children and has no time for fun and games. People adore her at work, and avoid her at home. It is as if she is taking off the super-hero costume and leaving it at the office. That's sad because it could be a key to finding more happiness at home.

Liz—and all of us—could take some direction from Coach Poyfair, who blurred the line between personal and professional, approaching every team in his life—even girls' soccer—with the same Orange perspective.

So what teams in your personal life could use a little Orange? If you don't think you're part of a team outside of work, think again. At our most basic level, human beings are pack animals. We naturally join together into groups for many reasons, including emotional fulfillment, safety, happiness, and social status. Below we've listed just a few of the team relationships that probably exist in your personal life, along with just a few benefits of such groupings:

- Marriages and committed relationships (love, support, finance, collaboration)
- Families (nurturing, management, mentoring, survival)
- Friendships (cheering, motivating, support, honesty)
- Communities (regulations, laws, ethics, standards, expectations)
- Neighborhoods (security, respect, goodwill)
- Schools (finance, management, mentoring, strategy)
- Volunteer work (charity, compassion, social betterment)
- Churches (guidance, support, leadership, guidance, respect)

If we accept this list, we realize that a lot is riding on our personal team-building skills. The most important relationships in our lives function smoothly (or not) depending on how we approach them. Fortunately, creating a breakthrough team in your personal life isn't that different from doing it at the office. We start by defining a clear big-picture goal, then we collectively commit to living the Rule of 3: We wow each other. We make sure there are no surprises. And we cheer. When these elements are in place, the rest takes care of itself.

THE BIG PICTURE

It's interesting to note that families—arguably the most important teams in our lives—are among the few organizations on earth that plod along year after year without overriding goals. Schools have goals. Community and volunteer groups would not exist without an overriding purpose; it's what holds them together. But how many families do you know that have shared goals? More often than not, our families remain undefined.

With this in mind, imagine our surprise when we entered the kitchen of a friend's house several years ago and found a large, handwritten poster on the refrigerator outlining the family's goals for the year. This wasn't a chore board for the week, but a long-term view of where they wanted to improve as a group by December 31 of that year.

It wasn't fancy. The goals were written on a piece of construction paper, and we had a mental picture of our respective families sitting down together to map out their direction for the year.

This family had put together three big goals. One was related to their school work, another to their church attendance, and the third one struck us: Bring our neighborhood together. Even more surprising was that they had the insight to list a behavioral goal of how to get there: Throw two parties this year. Listening to the voices and laughter and Christmas music pouring out of the room down the hall, we realized that the party we were attending that night was probably the final step in fulfilling this family's goal to be more connected to their neighbors.

What this family did was remarkable in its simplicity: they crossed the line and brought an Orange team perspective home in the form of goal setting.

Since then we've been more conscious of this idea. As a result, we've met more families who create mission statements each year. Some statements are serious and others more relaxed, like a family motto. It doesn't matter what form it takes, as long as it pulls you together behind one, two, or three core ideas. We've heard of mission statements ranging from, "Be thankful for what we have and what we can give to others," to "We're good sports," to our favorite: "Deny Everything" for a family who was notorious at pulling practical jokes.

Because of this, no matter what form the goal or goals take, the result is an enhanced sense of belonging, meaning, and common purpose—or, in other words, a greater sense of esprit de corps among the people we value most.

WOW EACH OTHER

If you want to hold up a family that modeled an intense shared commitment to a goal (at least in the beginning), it might have been John and Elizabeth Edwards. You'll recall that Edwards was a handsome young U.S. presidential hopeful seeking the Democratic Party nomination in 2008. His campaign was picking up speed when his wife, Elizabeth, was diagnosed with metastasizing cancer. The news was devastating. Everyone thought Edwards's run was over. But in a press conference, he announced that he would continue to seek the nomination. Elizabeth said she supported the decision because she wanted her children to learn that they did not have to give up their lives when faced with adversity.

Their popularity ratings soared. The country seemed captivated by the couple's strength and unity; and then the unthinkable happened. It was discovered that while his wife was supporting him and battling cancer, Edwards was having an affair. In the time it took to draft a public statement, John and Elizabeth's shared goal was ended. The public was understandably shocked, but mostly they wondered why a man who was admired by so many would have thrown it all away.

It is a complicated issue, of course, but Edwards himself admits that he was working harder to impress others than his own family. In other words, he forgot that the people he needed to wow most were Elizabeth and his children.

Edwards's public statement is revealing: "In the course of several campaigns, I started to believe that I was special and became increasingly egocentric and narcissistic."

Unchecked, the need for public validation can become an addiction, said American Orthodox Rabbi Shmuley Boteach. "Once you make a man's [or woman's] ego dependent not on the love he gets from his family, but on the adoration he gets from the crowds, he transfers the locus of his self-esteem away from his intimate circle to a fickle public."

While we'd all probably agree that great achievements require focus, our research shows great *teamwork* requires a positive focus on our immediate team members—or things get off track. A husband and wife research team at Duke University asked subjects to name someone they saw as controlling their lives and someone they thought wanted them to have fun. Subjects then were required to solve complex problems, in the form of jumbled words, while those names flashed subliminally on a screen. You can probably guess what happened. The subjects performed substantially better when they were subliminally exposed to the name of the person who wanted them to have fun versus the person who exerted undue influence over them.

In other words, we thrive when we know others have our happiness at heart, and in turn we must be genuinely happy for those on our personal teams, especially when they are attempting to wow. Clearly, impressing our families and the members of our other personal teams—valuing their acknowledgment above all others—serves two important purposes: First, it keeps us from getting sidetracked and unconsciously derailing our primary goals; and, second, it measurably boosts our personal-team performance and commitment.

Coach Poyfair seemed to know this. When his fledgling team lost the first few games, in the crowd's or the other coach's eyes the Arsenal Strikers were living up to low expectations. But the coach wasn't listening. Instead, he turned his focus inward to his team, and together he and his girls redefined each game as a success. They weren't denying the fact that they lost the games, but to them, the final score wasn't as important as improving individually and as a team. Together, knowing they valued each other above the points on the board, they achieved something no one else thought possible.

The wow factor worked for the soccer players. It worked for Edison. And it can work in our families and other personal teams as we learn to impress each other.

A friend has an example. Despite her limited resources, a few years ago she surprised her daughter on her birthday with a day trip to a theme park. They caught an early morning flight to California on a low-budget airline, then took the bus to the park. The weather was cool and the lines were short. Talk about a wow experience.

But by late afternoon the fairy tale ended abruptly. She called the airline to check on their evening flight home and found it had been postponed until morning. An operator at this no-frills carrier listed a multitude of reasons why they weren't liable to pay for a hotel.

She was angry. She and her daughter were stuck with nowhere to stay. But her daughter redefined the moment, saying how thrilled she was to have more time at the park with her mom.

A realization washed over our friend as she remembered the goal of the trip: time together. Here was a chance to enjoy some one-on-one with her daughter. How many more chances like this would they have in their lives? So she put away her cell phone, and they rode every ride in the park until closing time.

They walked into the lobby of a hotel near midnight. The front desk admitted they were full, but considering the circumstances they vowed to find them a room for the night. They did, though it stretched her limited finances even further. But as this mom tucked her exhausted, joyous daughter into bed, she realized she would work as many extra shifts as necessary to make up the cost for this wow.

"Financially it was a disaster. But three years later, it's one of my best memories. The other day, I walked into my daughter's room, and she had dug up a picture of us at the hotel that night. I don't know where she found it, but she had it pinned up over her bed," she said. "I'd pay a whole lot more than I did to create that kind of memory for my girl."

NO SURPRISES

If you've seen the movie *The Incredibles*, you are familiar with the cartoon family in their stretchy red jumpsuits with black piping. Before *The Incredibles* discovered and defined their unique abilities, they were as discouraged and dysfunctional as any family on earth. The kids picked on each other. Dad was demoralized in his job and kept secrets from his wife. Mom and Dad argued about this and that. Who would have thought they had the ability to become a great team?

In true Hollywood form, however, they made a remarkable transformation in an hour and half. Everything changed when they started exploring their abilities. They learned to be honest with each other, even if it was hard. They began to trust. And while certainly simplified for the silver screen, they showed us a glimpse of the power of No Surprises in a personal team.

Let's return to the office for some guidance. In our 200,000-person survey conducted by HealthStream Research, leaders who were considered most effective by their teams demonstrated the following traits:

- They set measurable goals.
- They answered questions truthfully and directly.
- They listened respectfully to others.
- They were available when colleagues or employees needed to talk.
- They created an environment where employees felt free to express their views.
- They accepted and valued others' ideas.

While that list may seem simple, the attributes are tremendously effective (yet uncommon) in the workplace. Let's apply them now to our families and personal teams. To be considered effective we must define expectations; we must answer questions; we should listen, be available, and create an open environment; and finally, we should learn to accept ideas from others. When we take the time to do these things in our personal lives, we establish an environment where our team members feel like informed partners, so there are no (unpleasant) surprises. When we don't invest the time to define our roles and communicate expectations, we risk getting sidelined.

In our focus groups for this book, we asked for examples of communication gone awry in business people's personal lives. One woman recounted a tale. At work, Shannon said she knew better than anyone the chaos that can ensue when frequent and direct communication was neglected. But this busy woman was also the volunteer director of a youth group. In this role, Shannon coordinated the efforts of several adult volunteers who planned weekly service and outdoor activities for at-risk kids in the community. One adult was assigned to each age level, while it was Shannon's job to keep an eye on the program as a whole.

Barbara volunteered one fall and was assigned to the youngest group of kids. Shannon and Barbara met for a minute at their church one Sunday. Shannon handed her newest volunteer a stack of papers and wished her luck with her group. "Email if you have any questions," she said.

It quickly appeared, however, that Barbara was a flake. As the weeks passed, it was Shannon who would receive calls from kids or parents assigned to Barbara's group. They asked about the next activity, where they should meet, what they should bring. These kids, who needed special attention, had no idea what was going on and often didn't hear from their leader until minutes before an activity.

Not wanting the spark a confrontation, Shannon admitted she began quietly inviting these younger kids to join an older group. Barbara's group got smaller and smaller. Shannon thought she was being helpful; her volunteer saw it differently. Barbara's resentment bubbled over on the sidewalk outside the church one afternoon.

"Hindsight is 20/20, and I can see that I was wrong," said Shannon. "I thought I was avoiding conflict. I was supposed to be in charge, but I was not communicating clearly. Barbara did actually have the ability to take care of things; she just didn't understand the expectation. As a leader, I had never been clear about what she should or shouldn't do."

The catch is: real communication takes time. Rome wasn't built in a day, and neither is understanding and trust among team members. And most of us try to squeeze meaningful communication into just a few minutes a day.

A recent British survey of three thousand families shows

that most of us have just forty-five minutes of unscheduled time together daily, and that obviously isn't enough time to create a conducive environment for effective communication, even if we were all paying attention. But according to the researchers, most of us spend this precious time together eating and watching TV, or doing both at the same time. Only 3 percent of families read together and just 2 percent help each other with homework. Yet the strongest families use their time together wisely. They take walks, support each other at their sporting or music events, talk daily about their challenges and successes, play games, learn new things, and so on.

Clearly, for the most part, we're not communicating effectively with our family members. Part of the problem is our focus. The same survey showed that parents were twice as likely to identify themselves as "TV and digital families" as "caring families." Obviously gone in many homes is the priority to look after each other's well-being. Case in point: when asked what was keeping them from spending more time with their children, parents listed long working hours, household chores, and spending time with friends. Finding time for communication with the most important people in our lives is a matter of priorities. The question is: Can chores, golf, or our friends wait?

If we want our families to do incredible things, we have to know each other well enough to be open. We must learn to trust and be trusted, and we must commit to a culture of no surprises. Like love, you can't hurry the process. It takes time.

CHEER FOR EACH OTHER

Back to the soccer field and Coach Poyfair. This neophyte instructor created a perfect storm for an Orange Revolution. The girls had a common *goal*. They *wowed* each other more and more as the season progressed. They sat together regularly at practices to talk and learn, so on game day there were *no surprises* about what was expected of a contributing team member. But what really activated the Arsenal Strikers' potential, what really set them on fire, was consistent, timely recognition. They *cheered* for each other.

Using common sense, it's not hard to understand why this is important. In our surveys of employees and managers we've trained around the world, more than 95 percent say they perform at a higher level when their contributions are acknowledged. Chances are in your past, a teacher or parent recognized something you did well and sparked to you to achieve more. Perhaps they appreciated your knack for science, ear for music, flair for writing, athletic prowess, sense of humor, leadership, or sense of style. With a mark on a paper or a comment with a smile they triggered a response that helped you believe in yourself, and caused you to repeat and even improve your behavior. Perhaps it helped you focus so intently on your attribute that it led to a career choice.

Others feel equally touched when they're cheered for. Our research *proves* that recognition is a driver of human performance. It is one of the few behavioral sciences where we can use the word "proved," because it has been statistically shown over and over to accelerate the performance and engagement of children, teens, adults, frontline workers, managers, and members of executive teams worldwide. But it's more than that. People also respond favorably to witnessing their team members receive frequent, specific, and timely recognition—they want to emulate the person being recognized.

So when Coach Poyfair publicly praised one girl, he was actually motivating all of them. When he awarded a Garrett the Carrot, all the girls watching the presentation were silently vowing to be the next one to hear the cheering, and figuring out how to emulate the things that the girl was doing right.

The same thing has been happening with the U.S. Olympic Ski Team over the past few years. Andy Lane, a professor of sports psychology at Wolverhampton University, explained that after placing a stronger emphasis on providing positive feedback to each other, the skiers reported a boost to their self-esteem and confidence. In addition, individual team member's performances have improved—as was evidenced at the 2010 Olympic Winter Games.

Here's one last example outside the business world. Just before the 2009 fall season, Ted Priestly took over as the men's soccer coach at Holy Cross, a liberal arts college in Worcester, Massachusetts. Priestly knew he needed to inspire a group of players who, quite frankly, resembled many companies today—teams with good potential but sagging returns.

The players he inherited started slow, losing six of their first seven games. But Coach kept teaching his system and kept recognizing his players' above-and-beyond efforts, knowing those two things would eventually turn the tide. Said Priestly, "We're big on recognition. Our guys learned that we compete during practice to win a starting position. But if a player loses the battle for a position, we expect him to be cheering for his teammates on game day."

It's a philosophy that the hard-nosed coach admits he came to grudgingly. "I had Orange phobias. I was afraid that I would reward too much, that the players would come to expect it and it would devalue the reward and the praise. I'd made the mistake early on as a coach saying, 'They don't need a pat on the back. They don't need recognition.' But I realized that I like a pat on the back too. I like motivation. I like recognition. High achievers are recognition sponges."

So while the critics were circling during those dark early days of the season, Coach Priestly kept recognizing. And something good happened. The Crusaders started winning. "When I asked the guys what was the biggest difference between the beginning of the season where we had more losses, and the end of the season where we fell just one game short of the playoffs, they all said the same thing: We finally bought into the system."

It's a system that has cheering as a foundation. In fact, as a constant reminder of the need to appreciate, Priestly even outfits his Holy Cross goalkeepers in orange. "Any manager, if nothing else, needs to ensure that the person on the other end feels special, feels appreciated, and feels important to the success of the group," he added.

But such cheering is not just for sports teams. Families, neighbors, civic groups, and many others can root for their fellow members. As an exercise, take note of the ways you can recognize your neighbors, friends, and family members in the coming week. Entries may include:

To a teacher: "That multiplication game you sent home has really helped Kellie. Thanks for taking the time to find something that worked for her. She went from hating math to it being a favorite. You really make a difference."

To a grocery bagger: "You always put the bread and fruit and eggs in separate bags so they don't get squished. Not everyone does that. Thanks."

To a Scoutmaster: "Thanks for keeping Tony going with his merit badges. He got discouraged but you wouldn't let him give up. We are so grateful you kept in touch every week to see how he was progressing."

To a significant other: "I really appreciate you coming with me to my work party. I know you don't know anyone here, but it means a lot to have you with me."

To a teenage neighbor: "I noticed that you've been driving slow on our street and watching for the kids. You are really thoughtful."

To a niece: "I saw you hold the door open for that other girl. That was really kind."

To the dry cleaner: "You know, I come here because my clothes are always on time. And if I have a problem, you take care of it right away. You're amazing."

We could go on, but you get the idea. It just takes a moment to recognize someone in a specific way, but the impact on the future is undeniable. That's because recognition:

1. Defines exactly what behaviors you value (unsquished zucchini, starched shirts, careful driving, etc.); and
2. Makes the recipient feel their efforts are noticed, motivating them to repeat those behaviors.

Such cheering combines clarity of purpose with a strong emotional reaction in a way that nothing else can. And it gives us the power to revolutionize the personal teams that matter most to us.

After all, teams are everywhere. They cross the line between home and office. We rely on them to fulfill our most basic human needs. So it just makes sense to put our best relationship tools to work where they matter most. As we set clear goals and commit to the Rule of 3 we bring the Orange Revolution home. And this time, it's *personal*.

11

The Orange Formation

W e'd like to tell one last story of great teamwork. It's a good one.

Bob Day is an executive with Cargill Grain & Oilseed Supply Chain business in China. Cargill, an international producer and marketer of food, agricultural, financial, and industrial products and services, is one of the world's largest private companies, employing more than 159,000 people and reporting more than $120 billion in annual sales. Day told us recently about a late autumn canoe trip he took with his former college fraternity buddies in Quetico Provincial Park, just west of Thunder Bay, Ontario, Canada. "We take the trip annually to escape the stress of modern life," said Day.

On their final day in the park, as the men took down their tents and loaded the canoes for the four-hour paddle back to a more civilized world, Day looked to the sky to see a beautiful display of nature. There, in the distance, at least a hundred Canadian geese had just launched themselves into the morning sky. Within seconds the geese were flying in V-formation—perfectly spaced. Although the gray horizon seemed vast and unending, the geese disappeared into the distance almost as quickly as they appeared—obviously headed for a more desirable climate.

Day thought about the duties shared between himself and his fraternity brothers throughout the week. He thought about the organization and planning of the trip, the shared responsibilities needed to paddle, catch fish, gather firewood, chop wood, cook, and clean the dishes. He thought about the fact that every day his rag-tag team had to overcome differences and natural self-interest to find a way to work toward a common goal—a campfire-cooked meal that could only be the product of the entire group. Watching the geese disappear into the distance, Day wondered, "What could we learn from those birds?"

Scientists, throughout the years, have presented theories of why migratory birds such as geese fly in a V-shaped formation. Not long ago, a team of scientists from Centre National de la Recherche Scientifique, in Villiers en Bois, France, was given a unique opportunity to study great white pelicans that had been trained to fly behind aircraft and motorboats for a feature film. These French scientists found that the birds' heart rates decreased when they were flying together and they were able to glide more often—reducing the energy they exerted during their migration journey.

Their work suggests that formation flight evolved because it allows birds to reduce their energy expenditure and fly farther—a near 70 percent increase in distance before stopping to rest. Birds flying in a V also had lower heart rates than birds flying alone. The aerodynamic V formation reduces the air resistance that each bird experiences—compared with a bird flying solo. This allows the animals to cover longer distances with much less effort.

Of course, in the V formation, the bird in the lead position will experience a greater air resistance and will have to work harder than the others. But this is where the formation process is remarkable. When the bird in front tires, it falls out of the lead and allows another bird to take over. This exchange takes only a second or two, barely evident from the ground, and is a feat of maneuverability that would make our Blue

Angel friends green with envy. The process—one bird flying in the lead until it becomes exhausted—continues throughout the migratory journey. Each bird takes a turn in front, because each has strength to give.

The formation allows all birds to benefit individually while working harmoniously as a team. And to Bob Day, watching the geese that morning, it was a demonstration of how teamwork plays a very important and useful role in nature and in business—reaching a goal by combining strengths, efforts, and a common understanding.

Just minutes into their paddle back to civilization, Day and his group witnessed a second formation of geese take flight. Day told us that all six men stopped paddling at that point to watch the magnificence of nature pass above them. The sounds were haunting: small ripples of water lapping against the sides of the drifting aluminum canoes and the honks of the geese that echoed through the tall pines and skipped across the seemingly endless dark waters.

In the canoe, Day wondered, "How far will the birds make it today? Where will they rest? When will they reach their final destination for the winter?"

He asked: "How many people will stop paddling, driving, talking, complaining, and competing when they see those geese—a symbol of perfect synergy—pass above them?" and "What is the ripple effect of such inspiration?"

"No one spoke when those geese launched into perfect formation," said Day. "As a manager—one who has always understood the value of teamwork—I wanted to capture that moment and share that innate understanding with my team at Cargill."

He continued, "I am amazed at how the flock leverages every bird to maximize its flying potential. By allowing each bird to lead the 'V' for a time, they are in effect eliminating that bird's weakness, and therefore have no weak link in the chain. The parallel in business is entrusting different people to lead the many initiatives and supporting tasks, aligning skill sets with specific responsibilities."

Day says that since that canoe trip he has become more aware of his own leadership philosophies at Cargill—that even though he had always believed in creating strong teams, the formation of the geese provides an invaluable model.

"So much of team success depends upon strong leadership," he says. "However, the actual role of the leader is often misunderstood. A good manager and leader is one who spends energy building and developing a strong team instead of always trying to lead from the front. If the strongest bird always led, it would get tired and the flock wouldn't get nearly as far. I find I'm most effective when I spend my time coaching and teaching instead of leading all the initiatives. In the end it is the strength of the team that matters."

Day's right, of course. Effective teams set in motion a complex chain of events that impact the entire organization and in some cases the world around them. They change the process, the systems, the outcomes, and the expectations forever. Each team—constructed of many variable personalities—influences progress that cannot often be forecasted. And yet each team formation will choose a slightly different, innovative flight pattern.

These things we do know about such team revolutions: As members commit to a shared goal, they are able to focus on what matters most to the organization and each other. That commitment generates a dedication to produce world-class results and the need for unrestrained honesty—an agreement to back each other up with no surprises. And members of great teams learn to genuinely cheer for each other. They do not root because it seems like a nice thing to do, but because they've actually become one single, codified unit.

On a great team, members don't consider themselves one of five, for instance, but one-fifth of one. With this awakening, team leaders witness a transformation. They learn the importance of sharing the credit, and allowing ownership. They learn to cultivate and promote the assets of their team—setting the team free to soar. And it is here in the launch of possibility where all team members truly engage and commit to the work, goal, or task at hand. They are willing to do more than just "put in time." Instead, they invest talent, courage, creativity, effort, and passion—all geared toward winning together.

This is the Orange Revolution. It's about getting into a powerful formation and taking the journey that will lead you and your team far beyond your wildest expectations.

Appendix

The Research

At the end of 2009, we enlisted the help of an independent research firm to prepare one of the largest-ever reports on teamwork. This new data would allow us to see to what extent the personal attributes of the Basic 4 + Recognition are found in revolutionary teams, and would give us insights into the role team affiliation plays in creating a great workplace and inspiring regular people to become great players.

The research was culled from the 350,000-person database of Harrisburg, Pennsylvania-based Best Companies Group (BCG), which works with partners throughout the United States and Canada to establish "Best Places to Work" programs. BCG's database comprises more than 350,000 people: 117,000 were interviewed in 2008 and 240,000 in 2009.

With the dramatic changes to the economy, new data was paramount. Thus the data we present in the graphs in this book is from 2009; however BCG compared the 2009 data with 2008 levels for corroboration—allowing us to validate these findings on the larger database. There was no statistically significant variation year over year in the results we present.

Employees from twenty-eight industries were studied— from accounting to government, health care to technology, financial services to education, services to manufacturing.

The bias was to use organizations of more than 250 employees, thus:

- 1 percent of respondents work for small companies (15–24 employees)
- 28 percent work for medium-sized companies (25–249 employees)
- 71 percent work for large companies (250+ employees)

Before we introduce the core of the findings, we did find an interesting variation in employee satisfaction by company size. We took this as the first validation for our team-camaraderie hypothesis: Despite the fringe benefits and security associated with working in a larger organization, employees working in small companies are more satisfied with their jobs overall than employees in larger companies. In fact, 91 percent of employees in small companies report being satisfied with their jobs compared with 82 percent in medium companies and 80 percent in large.

Employees of small companies generally report higher levels on attributes throughout the analysis. Medium-sized companies have the second most engaged employees, and large companies the least. Therefore, we see that when employees are able to connect with a smaller working team, they generally derive more satisfaction from their work, which is a learning that actually can be applied within larger organizations. These big companies can work to strengthen teams and departments, keep them together longer, and provide the tools and resources these teams need to succeed.

DATA OBJECTIVES

We asked BCG to identify what we called the Orange Revolution questions, ten questions from this large survey that reinforced the Basic 4 + Recognition. If our theory was right, these ten questions would be answered positively by team members who were seen by BCG as "engaged." And, in turn, if employees on a team answered the ten negatively, they would most likely show up as "disengaged" on the BCG rolls.

The questions were organized as shown. Respondents were asked to rate their level of agreement with the following:

Orange Revolution Questions	
Goal Setting	• I understand the long-term strategy of this organization • There is adequate planning of departmental objectives
Communication	• This organization's corporate communications are frequent enough • Changes that may affect me are communicated to me prior to implementation • Leaders of this organization are open to input from employees
Trust	• I feel I can trust what this organization tells me
Accountability	• There is adequate follow-through of departmental objectives • I am given enough authority to make decisions I need to make
Recognition	• This organization gives me enough recognition for work that is well done • My supervisor acknowledges when I do my work well

MEASURING SATISFACTION
AND ENGAGEMENT

In compiling a Best Places to Work list, BCG asks dozens of questions that measure employee opinions on all aspects of the work experience, from leadership to planning to work environment to pay and benefits. However, BCG has identified five areas that are most likely to indicate an engaging team environment:

- Overall employee satisfaction
- Likelihood of employee to recommend employment to a friend
- Likelihood of employee to recommend the company's products and services
- Likelihood of employee to remain employed at least two more years
- Willingness of employee to give extra effort when asked

Employees who agree or strongly agree to questions relating to the five ideas above are most likely engaged and the team they are working on could be considered outstanding. These employees are willing to take ownership of problems; provide innovation and ideas; have a desire to contribute to the success of their fellow teammates; and have an emotional bond to the organization, its mission, and its vision.

BCG's analysis showed that the ten Orange Revolution questions do have a significant impact on its five criteria for an engaged workplace.

Let's start with satisfaction.

As background, we measure satisfaction to help us understand employee motivators and to predict employee retention. Satisfaction is not employee engagement, and vice versa. While the two certainly reinforce and complement each other, there's value in studying both. Satisfied employees may come to work and do their jobs, but may not work at their highest capacity if they are not engaged. On the other hand, an employee may be highly engaged to do great work but dissatisfied with pay, management, or resources. Thus, such employees are a flight risk. Focusing on the development of both satisfaction and engagement contributes to higher customer satisfaction, reduces turnover, increases productivity, and improves profits.

We were pleased to find team member satisfaction increased steadily and dramatically as study participants favorably answered more Orange Revolution questions. Only 12 percent of teammates indicate they are satisfied with their work environment when none of the key questions are answered with "agree" or "strongly agree." However, the vast majority of employees (92 percent) are satisfied when all questions are answered favorably. This pattern holds true regardless of company size, industry, and whether or not a company made or missed making a BCG list.

Overall Satisfaction

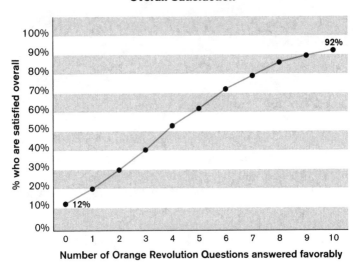

Another key driver of an engaging team environment as identified by BCG is an employee's likelihood to recommend employment to a friend or family member. This rating increases dramatically as more Orange Revolution questions are answered favorably: only 23 percent of employees indicate they are likely to recommend an acquaintance hire on when no key questions are answered favorably, while almost everyone (99 percent) is likely to recommend when all ten key questions are answered positively.

Likelihood to Recommend Employment

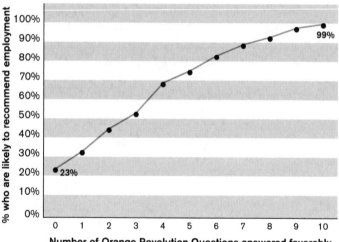

We also noticed an encouraging trend with the number of Orange Revolution questions and an employee's willingness to recommend his company's products and services. Less than four in ten team members (38 percent) are willing to recommend when no key questions are answered favorably, compared with 99 percent when all are answered favorably. Basically, an Orange Revolution can drive sales.

Notice on this analysis how quickly a team member's willingness to recommend his company's wares increases when just a few key questions are answered positively: 83 percent of employees agree or strongly agree when just four questions are answered favorably.

Likelihood to Recommend Products/Services

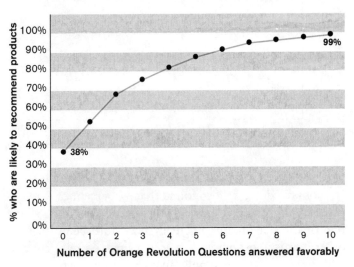

The way to measure employee turnover on this type of survey is by asking if a person intends to leave his or her team. We noted that team members become steadily more likely to remain as the number of favorable answers to the Orange Revolution questions increases. Some 40 percent of people wish to stay when no key questions are answered favorably, while 97 percent want to remain employed at least two years when all key questions are answered in the affirmative. These numbers varied little from 2008 to 2009, illustrating the deteriorating economic climate has had little impact on the predictors of turnover. A strong workplace will keep people and keep them engaged. Period.

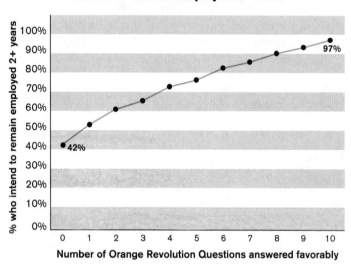

Intend to Remain Employed 2+ Years

From the data, we also found that 57 percent of employees are willing to give extra effort—even when not a single one of the personal competency needs are being met. In other words, most employees accept that commitment and additional effort are simply an expectation in the strong organizations BCG studies. After all, in this economy most of us jump when the boss says jump. But look what happens when just two of the ten Orange Revolution questions are answered favorably by team members: the number of people willing to give extra effort increases from 57 percent to 82. And with all questions answered positively, an almost unanimous 99 percent of teammates report they'd give more when needed.

Willing to Give Extra Effort

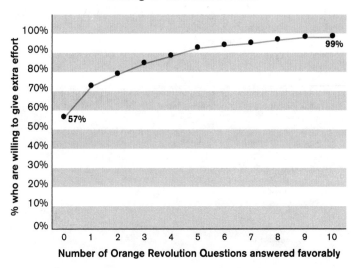

On an interesting side note, our researchers used regression analysis to evaluate the effectiveness of the Orange Revolution questions in predicting responses to the query, "Overall, how satisfied are you with your company as an employer?" As you can see from the chart on the next page, employees who were satisfied with their team and their company are clearly more likely to feel these Orange needs are being met. But what is interesting is the order of importance to satisfaction: Trust was most important in driving such morale, goal-setting second, communication third, accountability fourth, and recognition fifth.

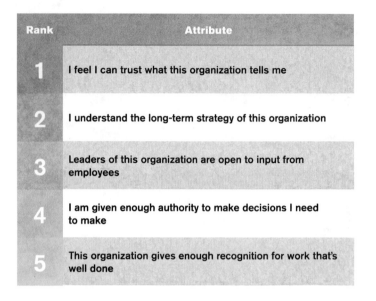

Rank	Attribute
1	I feel I can trust what this organization tells me
2	I understand the long-term strategy of this organization
3	Leaders of this organization are open to input from employees
4	I am given enough authority to make decisions I need to make
5	This organization gives enough recognition for work that's well done

WHAT MAKES A GREAT ORGANIZATION?

Finally we asked the researchers to cut the data so we could identify differences between organizations that made a Best Places to Work list and those good firms that wanted to be included but missed the cut. It's important to remember that these are all very solid organizations, companies that believed they were good enough to receive the acclaim of being on a "Best Places to Work" list.

What arose from the data were several interesting statistical variances related to the ideas of teamwork and camaraderie. Here's the difference for teamwork:

As you can see, in companies that made a Best Places to Work list, 90 percent of employees feel they are part of a team working toward a shared goal. In those good organizations that tried but failed to make a list, only 80 percent of employees agreed that they have a shared team commit-

Teamwork

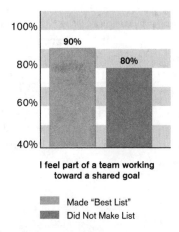

I feel part of a team working
toward a shared goal

Made "Best List"
Did Not Make List

ment to their goals. (One must only assume that average or poor companies would report even lower teamwork numbers, though we didn't include such organizations in this analysis).

Next, we looked at camaraderie.

Camaraderie

I believe there is a spirit of
cooperation at this organization

Made "Best List"
Did Not Make List

Note here that in companies that made a Best Places to Work list, 90 percent of employees feel there is shared camaraderie. In those good organizations that tried but failed to make a list, only 77 percent feel there is camaraderie.

A delta of this magnitude provides a wonderful exclamation point to this idea of teamwork, and offers us some understanding of what it takes to be great. In the strongest organizations, leaders and team members actively pursue the human side of their business. They spend time drawing teams together. They build a culture of caring. And all of that pays dividends.

NOTES

1: Breakthrough Teams

1 The story of Thomas Edison appears throughout the first few chapters. Sources include:
- Michael J. Gelb and Sarah Miller Caldicott. *Innovate Like Edison: The Success System of America's Greatest Inventor.* New York: Dutton, 2007.
- Neil Baldwin. *Edison: Inventing the Century.* New York: Hyperion, 1995.
- Randall Stross. *The Wizard of Menlo Park: How Thomas Alva Edison Invented the Modern World.* New York: Crown, 2007.
- John F. Wasik. *The Merchant of Power: Samuel Insull, Thomas Edison, and the Creation of the Modern Metropolis.* New York: Palgrave Macmillan, 2006.

4 John-Steiner's research can be found in: Vera John-Steiner, *Notebooks of the Mind: Explorations of Thinking,* 2d ed. Albuquerque, N.M.: Univ. of New Mexico Press, 1997.

8 The dramatic story of the crew of the HMAS Dechaineux was culled from:
- Cameron Stewart. "Submarine Crew was 20 Seconds from Death." *The Australian,* NSW Country Edition, December 26, 2008.
- Dan Box. "Sailors under Pressure." *The Australian,* All-round Country Edition, December 6, 2007.
- Cameron Stewart. "Sub-standard Back-up." *The Australian,* All-round Country Edition, February 2, 2009.

11 Vince Lombardi's quote was from: David Maraniss. *When Pride Still Mattered: A Life of Vince Lombardi.* New York: Touchstone, 2000.

12 Max Messmer's quote and the accompanying survey results are from: Stephanie Armour. "Friendship and Work: A Good or Bad Partnership?" *USA Today*, August 2, 2007

13 The Wharton and Gartner Group research was culled from: Lawrence G. Hrebiniak, "Business Strategy: Execution Is the Key," Wharton School Press, January 21, 2005.

14 The example of the steel mill was taken from: Richard Preston. *American Steel*. New York: Quill, 1992.

17 The obligatory interdependence concept came from: Marilynn B. Brewer, "The Importance of Being We: Human Nature and Intergroup Relations," *American Psychologist*, November 2007.

19 The claim that 40 percent of senior people in new roles fail is documented in: Michael Watkins. *The First 90 Days*. Boston: Harvard Business Press, 2003.

2: The Common Cause

22 General Washington's defining moment was courtesy of several sources, most notably:
- Terry Golway. *Washington's General: Nathanael Greene and the Triumph of the American Revolution*. New York: Holt, 2005.
- David McCullough. *1776*. New York: Simon & Schuster, 2005.

33 The dictator-by-default syndrome was outlined by: Bob Frisch. "When Teams Can't Decide," *Harvard Business Review*, November 1, 2008.

3: Competence: Back to the Basics (+ Recognition)

39 The survey on employee competitiveness was courtesy: Office Team, A Robert Half Company. "The Team's the Thing," August 13, 2008.

41 Worker incompetence data came from: Aubrey C. Daniels. "Reducing Employee Errors," *Entrepreneur*, March 4, 2002.

54 The University of Alberta study on eudaimonia was found in: "Secret to Workplace Happiness: Remember What You Love about the Job," a University of Alberta press release, November 26, 2008.

60 The work on trust's impact on an economy was culled from:

Paul J. Zak and Steven Knack, "Trust and Growth," September 18, 1998, as part of the Claremont Graduate University Center for Neuroeconomics Studies Working Paper Series.

66 The U.S. Department of Labor statistic can be found in many places, including: Matthew Kirdahy, "Why Is It So Hard to Say 'Well Done'?" Forbes.com, September 13, 2007.

4: The Rule of 3: Cultivating a Team

81 The paragraph on "loss of control" was improved with ideas from the following article: Saj-nicole Joni and Damon Beyer. "How to pick a good fight," *Harvard Business Review*, December 2009.

5: Wow: Six Secret Ingredients to World-Class Results

88 The iPod example was enhanced with various sources, including:
- Leander Kahney. *Inside Steve's Brain*. New York: Portfolio. 2008.
- Leander Kahney. *The Cult of iPod*. No Starch Press. 2005.
- Tom Koulopoulos. "iTunes innovation is about imagination, not dollars," Wisconsin Technology Network, May 14, 2008.
- "Apple CEO Steve Jobs Talks Exclusively to Fortune Magazine about His Plans," BusinessWire, April 28, 2003.
- Apple.com.
- Nationmaster.com Encyclopedia, found at statemaster.com/encyclopedia/Jon-Rubinstein.
- Brad Cook. "England's *Sunday Times* Names Jonathan Ive One of 25 Top Britons in America," The iPod Observer, November 27, 2005.

111 The story of Creed was highlighted with examples from:
- Creed.com.
- "Creed Break Up: Mark Tremonti blames tensions between band, singer Scott Stapp," MTV.com, June 4, 2004.
- "Creed to reunite in 2009," UltimateGuitar.com, December 2, 2008.
- Eddie Ruckus. "Creed Come Full Circle," Trimplem.com, September 15, 2009

6: No Surprises: Mastering Orange Communciation

120 Details about the Blue Angels were culled from our interviews with Scott Beare and from: Scott Beare and Michael McMillan. *The Power of Teamwork*. Simple Truths Publishing, 2006.

127 John C. Maxwell. *The 17 Essential Qualities of a Team Player: Becoming The Kind Of Person Every Team Wants*. Thomas Nelson, 2002.

7: Cheer: Up

144 The Lesson of 38 Chocolate Bars was provided to us by The New York Times, © August 8, 2008. All rights reserved. Used by permission and protected by the Copyright Laws of the United States. The printing, copying, redistribution, or retransmission of the Material without express written permission is prohibited.

8: 101 Ways to Bring Your Team Together

188 Tips for quieting loud voices were culled from: *Teams That Click*. Boston: Harvard Business School Press, 2004.

189 Toxic team member ideas were taken from: *Harvard Business School Press Pocket Mentor: Leading Teams*. Boston: Harvard Business School Publishing, 2006.

10: An Orange Life: A How-To Guide for Living

220 Some of the information about John Edwards came from: Shmuley Boteach, "Why Great Men like John Edwards Cheat," *The Huffington Post*, August 11, 2008.

221 The Duke University research was found in: Laura Brinn, "Nagging Spouse? You May Have an Excuse for Not Responding," a press release from the Duke University Office of News and Communication, February 13, 2007.

225 The time spent in front of the television statistics came from: Fay Schlesinger. "Most Family Time Spent in Front of TV," *The Advertiser*, May 28, 2009.

228 Information on the U.S. Ski Team came from: John Naish. "In This Together," *The Times* (London), January 5, 2008.

11: The Orange Formation

231 Information on the flight patterns of geese was culled from:
- "Bird flight explained," BBC News World Edition, December 16, 2002.
- Susan Huebert. "Urban wildlife in city parks and streams," suite101.com, July 31, 2009.

O.C. TANNER COMPANY

For more than 80 years, O.C. Tanner has helped companies appreciate great work—creating high-performance cultures where innovation, extra effort, and more effective leadership practices drive real business results. The company provides recognition solutions with services such as manager training, administration, and communication as well as thousands of name-brand award options. Headquartered in Salt Lake City, Utah, O.C. Tanner currently has 1,750 employees and serves companies worldwide with offices throughout North America as well as international headquarters in Ontario and London.

BEST COMPANIES GROUP

Best Companies Group is dedicated to establishing "Best Places to Work," "Best Companies," or "Best Employers" programs in an effort to single out companies that are superior in workplace excellence. BCG researches the dynamics and characteristics of great workplaces, analyzes the data, and produces a "Best Places to Work" distinction that will make the participating company, the selected region (or industry), and the local organizing partners proud. The very mission of BCG is to "identify and recognize" organizations that are leading the way in defining the employee experience of the twenty-first century.

ACKNOWLEDGMENTS

The ideas in this book began taking shape after a Sunday afternoon meeting with Scott O'Neil. Scott is one of the most powerful behind-the-scenes figures in sports, and the center point of chapter 4. Between kids running through his living room and healthy doses of laughter ringing through the house, he introduced us to his team's Rule of 3, helping structure the ideas that were ruminating in our minds on teamwork. We owe him our first debt of gratitude.

Peter Burke and his team at Best Companies Group provided the research that validated and refined the ideas we were considering, and we thank him and his team for their expertise and insights. We also appreciate our research teams at Towers Watson, as well as the research team at O.C. Tanner, for drawing new data from our survey.

This idea then took shape with our agent Kevin Small, who helped us define the cause of the book. He has provided a source of guidance and wisdom in the publishing world that we had lacked, and we love that he looks out for us. We thank Kevin and his amazing team including Becky Blackburn.

Our editor, Emily Loose at Simon & Schuster, had helped us craft a bestseller with *The Carrot Principle*, and we weren't about to put out another book without her. She immediately saw potential in the ideas in our proposal, and pressed us during the edit to create a better finished work using a combination of impressive brilliance, savvy knowledge of the needs of readers, and medieval torture devices (or so it seemed). We kid because we adore her work (and because it's true). We thank Emily and the team at Free Press, which includes Martha Levin, Susanne Donahue, Dominick Anfuso, Alexandra Pisano, Carisa Hayes, Nicole Kalian, Tom Dussel, Paul O'Halloran, Larry Satt, and many others. An ancillary part of our publishing team is our wonderful publicist Mark Fortier, who always wows us with his attention to detail, and ability to spread the word and make noise.

Much appreciation is due to the wonderful team members in the organizations we have quoted within these pages. Wherever we traveled in the world to find your stories, you were generous with your time, patient with our questions, and we were moved by your inspiring examples. You include:

Texas Roadhouse: GJ Hart, Dave Dodson, Travis Doster, Dee Shaughnessy, Kim Boerema, Wendy Ennis, and Joel Barragan.

Zappos: Tony Hsieh, Dr. David Vik, Alfred Lin, Liz Gregersen, Christa Foley, Maura Sullivan, Rob Siefker, Rebecca Ratner, Loren Becker, Robert Richman, Donavon Roberson, Jamie Naughton, and Jerry "The Mayor" Tidmore.

American Express: Kevin Cox, David Kasiarz, Rebecca Booth, Jim Dwyer, Robert Childs, Ken Chenault, Jose Irizarry, Holly Faccin, Dmitri Krassotkine, LeeAnn Strickler, Bob Sloane, Debbie Thomas, Ed Chee, Gary Woo, Kristina Kubat, Vineet Verma, Bruce Mann, Bonnie Severin, Mike Wagner, and Steve Kvam.

Pets at Home: Matt Davies, Ryan Cheyne, and Andrew Blaney.

Pepsi Beverages Company: Eric Foss, John Berisford, Kevin Pfeiffer, Mary Beth DeNooyer, Steve Stalder, John Thibodeau, and Rajendra "Guru" Gursahaney.

Medical City: Virginia Rose (and her Posse) and former CEO Britt Berrett.

Thornton's: Matt Thornton and Tony Harris.

Sutherland Global Services: Robert Barclay and Jennifer Case.

U.S. Foodservice Inc.: Stuart Schuette, Christina Koliopoulos, Jody Hollister, Mark Eggerding, and Steve Horan.

Jumeirah Hotels and Resorts: Gerald Lawless and his team, and Mohammed Abdelhay at FranklinCovey Middle East for arranging an introduction.

Friendly Ice Cream Corporation: Ned Lidvall and Cheryl Hutchinson.

Nash Finch: Alec Covington, Michael Rotelle, Tonya Welsh, and Kathleen Mahoney.

Wynn Resorts: Arte Nathan and Steve Wynn.

Whirlpool Canada: Karim Lalani, Sue Promane, and Susan Koruna.

Sincere thanks also go to Blue Angels: Scott Beare; Cargill: Bob Day; NBA: Chris Heck; Holy Cross: Ted Priestly; the crew of the HMAS *Dechaineux*; Newark Airport: Brice Fukumoto; Pan Pacific Hotel: Judd Garcia Tecson; State Farm: Kevin Smith; CTS: Chris Carmichael.

We are fortunate to have some of the world's most talented teams working with us. We start with our internal team of Andrea Gappmayer, Andrew Hahn, Angie Haugen, BobAnn Hall, Joel Bishop, Christy Chatelain, Kim Coxey, Pat Poyfair, Scott Christopher, Stephanie Rodriguez, Steve Gibbons, and Bryan Rosenvall. We then thank our researchers and critical readers Glen Nelson, Todd Nordstrom, and Christie Giles. We also appreciate Ryan Forsthoff's experts at the Center for Great Management, including Ben Ortlip, Danny Jones, Clark Orr, and Justin Romine.

We would also be remiss if we didn't express gratitude to the entire O.C. Tanner Company, including Dave Petersen,

Carolyn Tanner Irish, Kaye Jorgensen, Tim Treu, John McVeigh, Gail Bedke, Brian Katz, Gary Petersen, David Sturt, Christina Chau, Mindi Cox, Shauna Raso, Jarond Suman, and many others who support this work.

The book is dedicated to our most important teams: To Jennifer and Tony. To Heidi, Cassi, Carter, Brinden, and Garrett.

INDEX

Orange Revolution Resources

Want to start an Orange Revolution in your team?

Login to receive the free tools that will help you and your team excel. Plus, get exclusive insight from some of the world's most recognized Orange Teams.

Visit carrots.com/orange
to get these free resources.

The Orange White Paper: Teamwork and Your Bottom-line

The hard data your boss needs: statistical evidence about the characteristics of Breakthrough Teams, and how these teams can accelerate performance and boost your bottom-line.

Weekly Esprit de Corps: Fresh Cheering Ideas in Your Inbox

We all could use some great ideas to bring our teams together. The Weekly Orange e-idea offers the latest thinking in creating breakout team results.

Film #1: Wow

Go inside one of the world's most talked-about retailers with Gostick and Elton, and learn how great teams structure themselves to deliver world-class results.

Film #2: No Surprises

Follow Gostick and Elton as they take an up-close look at a sky-high performance team, teaching us all lessons about open communication.

Film #3: Cheer

Join the authors as they examine one of America's fastest-growing restaurant chains, unveiling the secret recipe of effective cheering and recognition.

Visit carrots.com/orange **for your free resources.**

About the Authors

Adrian Gostick is the author of several bestselling books on corporate culture, including a *New York Times*, *USA Today* and *Wall Street Journal* bestseller *The Carrot Principle*. He also wrote the bestsellers *The Levity Effect* (levityeffect.com), *The Integrity Advantage*, and *The 24-Carrot Manager*. His research on employee engagement has been called a "must read for modern-day managers" by Larry King of CNN, "fascinating," by *Fortune* magazine, and "admirable and startling" by *The Wall Street Journal*.

Adrian's books have been translated into 20 languages and are sold in more than 50 countries around the world. As a leadership expert, he has appeared on numerous national television programs, including NBC's *Today* show and has been quoted in dozens of business publications and magazines.

Adrian is vice president of the Carrot Culture Group, a consulting and training division of the O.C. Tanner Company. Adrian earned a master's degree in Strategic Communication and Leadership from Seton Hall University, where he is a guest lecturer on organizational culture. You can reach him at adrian@carrots.com.

Called the "apostle of appreciation," by the *Globe and Mail*, Canada's largest newspaper, and "creative and refreshing" by *The New York Times*, Chester Elton is author of several bestselling leadership books. *The Carrot Principle* from Simon & Schuster has been a *New York Times*, *Wall Street Journal*, and *USA Today* bestseller, and *The 24-Carrot Manager* has been called a "must-read for modern-day managers" by Larry King of CNN. *The Invisible Employee*, from John Wiley & Sons, also appeared on the *New York Times* bestseller list. Elton's books have been translated into over 20 languages and have sold a million copies worldwide.

As a motivation expert, Chester has been featured in *The Wall Street Journal*, *The Washington Post*, *Fast Company* magazine, and *The New York Times*, and has been a guest on CNN, National Public Radio, and CBS' *60 Minutes*. A sought-after speaker and recognition consultant, Chester is the Senior Vice President of the Carrot Culture Group, a division of the O.C. Tanner Recognition Company.

Chester has spoken to delighted audiences from Seattle to Singapore and from Toronto to Istanbul. He was the highest-rated speaker at the national Society for Human Resource Management annual conference. He serves as a recognition consultant to Fortune 100 firms such as American Express, Wal-Mart, Pepsi Beverages Company, and Avis Budget Group. You can reach him at chester@carrots.com.

Orange Talk

During their travels the authors document the best team stories from around the world, gather the best how-tos on employee engagement, and interview some of the world's coolest business people to provide practical advice on what's working and what isn't. Their blogs are relevant, timely, and often hilarious.

ChesterElton.com

AdrianGostick.com